IMAGES
of America

ALPINE COUNTY
BEAR VALLEY, KIRKWOOD, AND MARKLEEVILLE

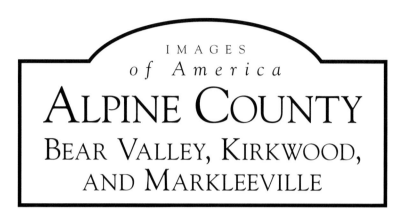

IMAGES
of America

ALPINE COUNTY
BEAR VALLEY, KIRKWOOD, AND MARKLEEVILLE

Alpine County Historical Society

ARCADIA

Published by Arcadia Publishing
Charleston SC, Chicago IL, Portsmouth NH, San Francisco CA

Printed in Great Britain

Library of Congress Catalog Card Number: 2005929123

For all general information contact Arcadia Publishing at:
Telephone 843-853-2070
Fax 843-853-0044
E-mail sales@arcadiapublishing.com
For customer service and orders:
Toll-Free 1-888-313-2665

Visit us on the internet at http://www.arcadiapublishing.com

CONTENTS

ACKNOWLEDGMENTS

This project could not have been done without the contribution of Dick Edwards, Alpine County Museum director. His unflagging effort procured the photographs from the museum archives, put them in a preliminary sequence so chapters could be developed, assisted with the writing and arrangement, and helped with layout and picture scanning for final production. Special acknowledgment is also due Bessie Platten, county librarian, who originally conceived the project, coordinated it through Arcadia Publishing, and assisted with the book's layout and organization of chapters. Particular thanks are due Karen Dustman, who researched and wrote the information for chapter two, Patty Brisbin, who researched and wrote chapter four, and Nancy Thornburg who provided text used in several chapters. A debt is also owed Gina Gigli, who helped with the layout and served as the line editor. The book profited from the efforts of Irving Krause, Ellen Martin, Lois Kaiser, Fritz Thornburg, and Gary Coyan, who assisted with research, gathered photographs, or verified historical information. The Alpine County Historical Society, the project sponsor, offers a sincere thank you to each of these individuals for their contribution.

—Michael J. Makley
President, Alpine County Historical Society

INTRODUCTION

Alpine County's development can be viewed as having three distinct periods. The first was the geologic development of the land and its features over the course of untold millennia. Internal disturbances caused the earth's surface to jut, fault, and explode, thrusting its crust outward, and external forces caused it to freeze and thaw, shaping it into its current form. During this time, evolving plants and animals competed in adapting to the land.

The second epoch began with the appearance of the Washo Indians. The Washo creation myth says that their people began here, and their Hokan language is evidence that they are among the oldest tribes in the Americas. For thousands of years their life cycle rotated with the seasons, living in these valleys during the winter and early spring, traveling to Lake Tahoe for the summer, and to the Pine Nut Mountains east of the Carson Valley in the fall. Their Eden provided them with fish, big and small game, acorn and pine nuts, and a large variety of medicinal and food plants. They saw themselves as caretakers of the land, air, water, and animals.

In May 1827, legendary mountain man Jedediah Smith, his pack animals dying, fought through winds and snow to cross what is now called Ebbetts Pass. Descending the summit, he made contact with the Washo, who disappeared after attempting to drive him away. This event signaled the initiation of the third period.

In the 1850s, a few Euro-Americans settled here. In the 1860s, gold and silver seekers, and those who produced food, services, and fuel for them, took up residence. This book intends to illustrate and illuminate the culture and lifestyle of this last age. Yet at the same time these photographs, taken from the Alpine County Museum collection, reflect the area's geologic wonders and the influence of its native people.

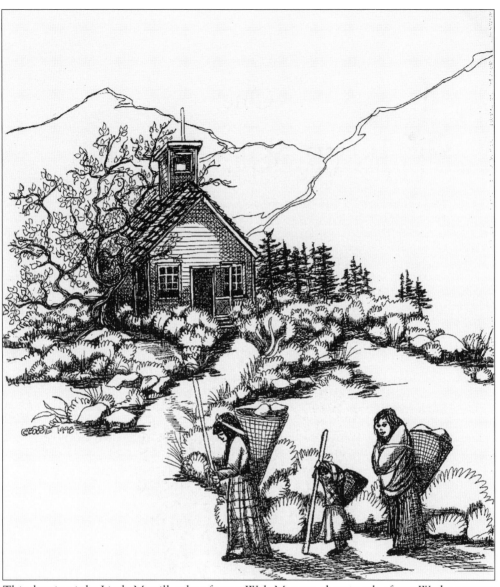

This drawing is by Linda Merrill, taken from a Walt Monroe photograph of two Washo women and a child walking up the hill to the Webster School.

One

THE WASHO PEOPLE

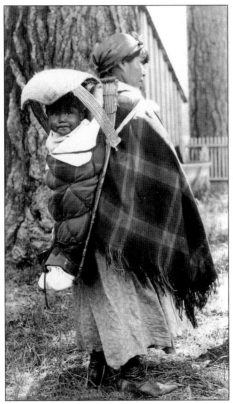

The Hung-a-lel-ti band is the southern branch of the Washo Indian tribe, living in what is now western Nevada and eastern California. When Euro-Americans came to their land, in the middle of the 19th century, there were perhaps 3,000 Washo spread from the valley of the Walker River in the south to Honey Lake in the north. For thousands of years, their cyclical lives had followed the seasons. They migrated to the sacred hub of their existence, Lake Tahoe, for the "Big Time" in the summer. In the fall they traveled to the Pine Nut Mountains, on the eastern side of present-day Carson Valley, Nevada, for the ceremony leading to the harvesting of piñon pine nuts, their staple food. The balance of each year, the Hung-a-lel-ti lived in family clans at valley home sites in Alpine County.

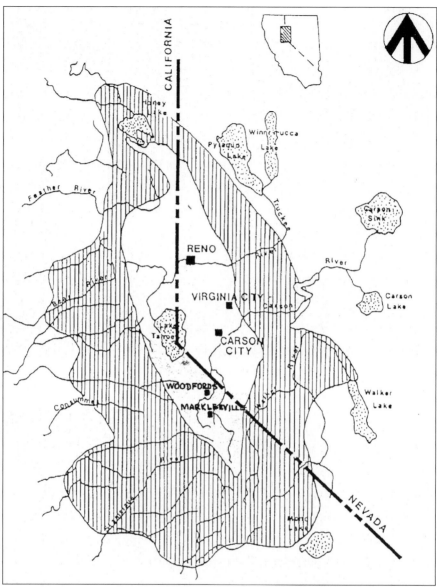

Much of the Washo diet was comprised of deer, antelope, rabbit, fish, pine nut seeds, and bulb plants. Washo hunted and fished alone or in small groups, but collecting pine nuts was a cooperative venture. Families or clans owned rights to wide strips of the piñon pine forest. During a month of intense activity in the fall, pine nuts were gathered. They were then carried to home sites and prepared. Gatherers knocked cones from the trees using a long pole, and the fallen cones were transported in burden baskets. Once removed, the seeds were cooked by various methods to prevent spoilage, and stored for use throughout the winter. In addition to gathering, hunting, and fishing, the Washo traded with the neighboring Paiute and Shoshone tribes to the east and the California tribes all the way to the Pacific Ocean to the west. Their Hokan-stock language is ancient, much older than those of neighboring tribes, evidence that they were probably the first aboriginals in this region. Washo mythology teaches that they were created here, and each stream, stand of rocks, or lake in the high country around Lake Tahoe is associated with their creation myth.

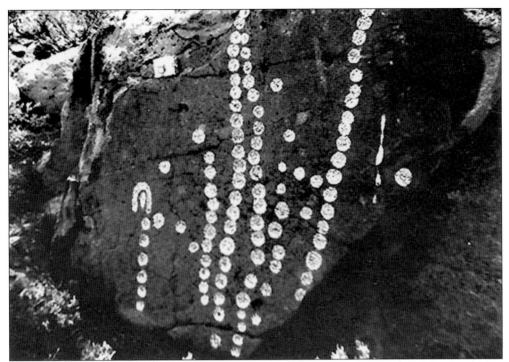

Petroglyphs near Big Spring on Monitor Pass were scratched into the rock more than 1,000 years ago. Some rocks were used over long periods of time, so that art styles from different periods are on the same surface.

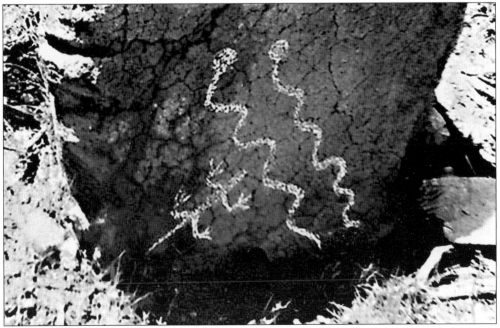

Rock art sites are located in areas where there are sloped, bare rocks. Some are at ancient home sites; others are where animal movements could be watched. The designs at right above could represent snakes or rivers, and a lizard at left. They are found at several sites.

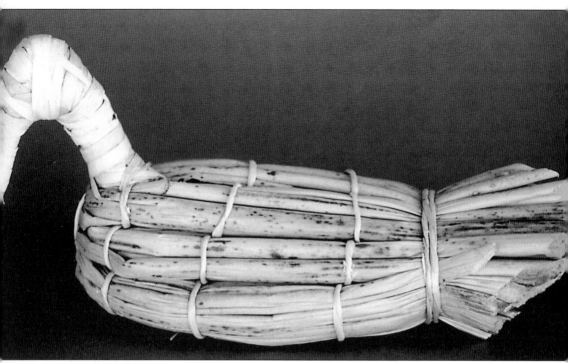

Tule duck decoys have been dated in this region to 2,500 years old. The decoys were made from the aquatic plant known as Cattail, *Typha gracilis*, found growing in moist waste areas and along streams and lakes. Martin George, of the Hung-a-lel-ti band, created the decoy seen here. He was the last in a long family line of decoy artisans that included his grandmother, the legendary Wuzzie George, who lived to be well over 100. Tragically, Martin died in 1994 at the age of 29. The body of the decoy was made from dampened stalks of cattail, and the head wrapped with the plant's slender leaves.

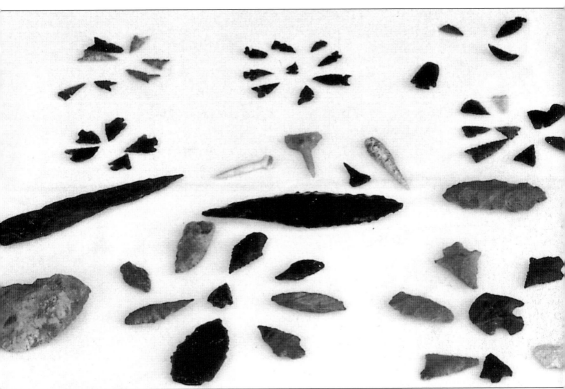

Members of the Hung-a-lel-ti were renowned for their use of the long bow, both for hunting and for keeping enemies at a distance. Bows were sinew-backed wood with strongly curved ends. Wooden arrows had delicately shaped obsidian or flint points attached by means of sinew bindings. Here a spearhead, an axe head, and a variety of arrowheads surround a stone knife and awls. The projectile points of the Washo in Alpine County were made of many different types of minerals. Obsidian was the preferred material for Native Americans across the United States, but in Alpine County it was scarce and had to be collected in Mono County to the south or traded from the Paiutes to the east. Local minerals, such as jasper and chert, were successfully used, although they did not have the volcanic flaking characteristics of obsidian, which can be sharpened to a surgically fine edge.

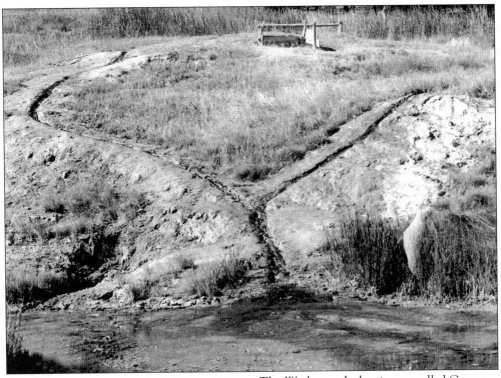

The Washo used what is now called Grover Hot Springs for centuries before Euro-Americans came to the area. Besides bathing in the springs, the Washo used the boiling water to soak deer hides to remove the hair and soften it as a part of the process of making buckskin. In 1967, Alpine County resident Harry Hawkins commented, "I've got some buckskins Hunter John made 60 years ago or better. They're just as soft as cloth."

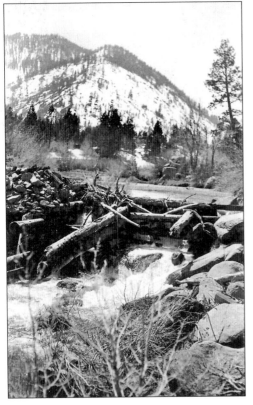

Fish resources were rich for the Hung-a-lel-ti. They ate white fish and trout, fresh or dried. Fishermen used two-pronged spears, nets, or hooks with angleworms, salmon eggs, and minnows as bait. The band built dams in small tributaries, diverting water to trap fish. Willow wands were woven into traps that blocked streams, or shaped into conical baskets for catching fish while wading.

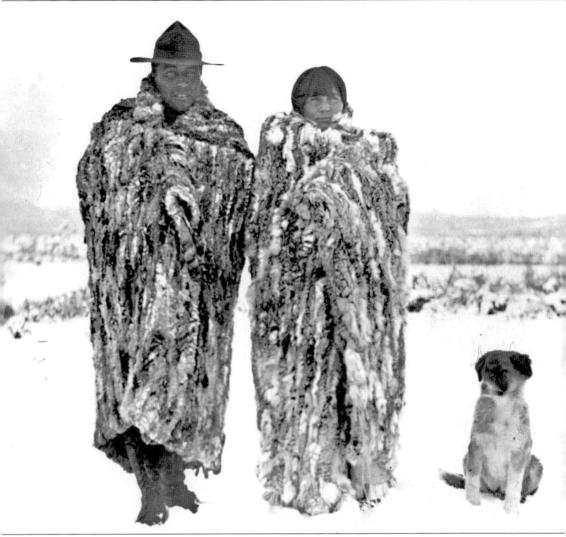

John and Wama Anthony are shown here wearing rabbit-skin robes. An adult-size robe was five feet square and required 24 skins. The Hung-a-lel-ti hunted rabbits in the late fall when their fur was thick. This most important article of clothing was light and warm, and served as a robe or blanket.

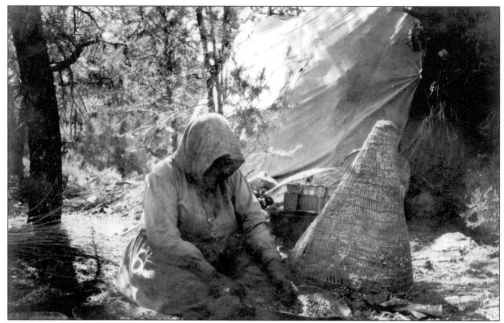

Pine nuts were stored for use throughout the year. Here an unidentified woman works with her winnowing basket.

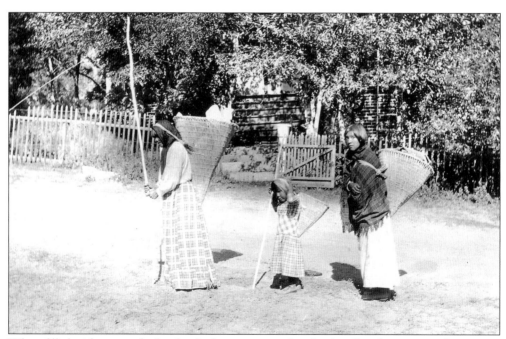

When filled with cones, the burden basket was carried with a headband or a trump line across the shoulders and chest, devices that kept hands free for carrying tools or weapons. These Washo, pictured *c.* 1920, walk across the junction of Highways 88 and 89 towards Woodfords Canyon.

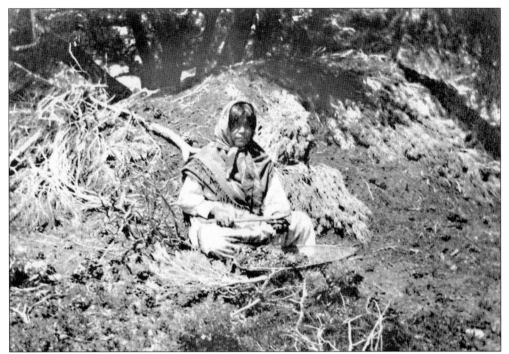

Susie Dick is seen here collecting pine nut seeds, *c.* 1910. The Pine Nut Mountains were a considerable walking distance from Alpine County home sites. In the autumn, families moved to the Pine Nuts for four to six weeks to collect the seeds. Cones were roasted until they opened enough for the nuts to be removed. The sweet, meaty nuts, when re-roasted, have a flavor resembling roasted almonds.

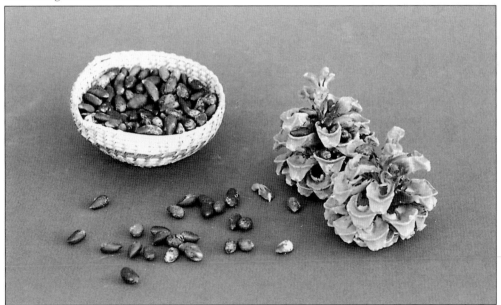

The Piñon Pine, *Pinus monophylla*, was the primary Washo source for pine nuts. They are found growing on the slopes of the eastern Sierra Nevada. Other varieties of piñon are found throughout the western United States.

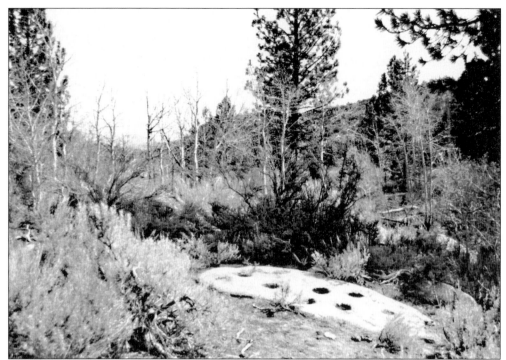

Each family collected literally tons of pine nuts yearly. They were ground into flour at sites like the one seen here in the Woodfords area. Cobblestone pestles or stone mullers were used to grind the seeds on flat-surfaced rocks.

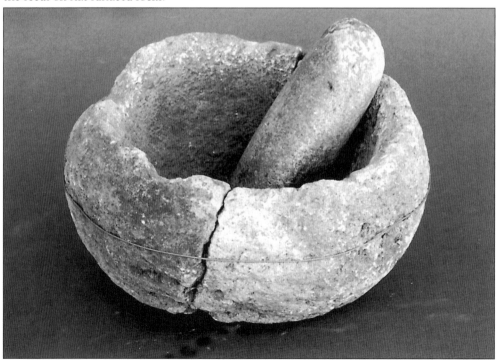

Certain foods and medicines, and face and body paint were ground in small, portable stone mortars.

Winnowing baskets were used to separate the pine nut meat from the shells. The crushed pine nuts were tossed from the basket into the air, the heavier nut meat falling back to the basket, and the breeze assisting to blow away the lighter shells.

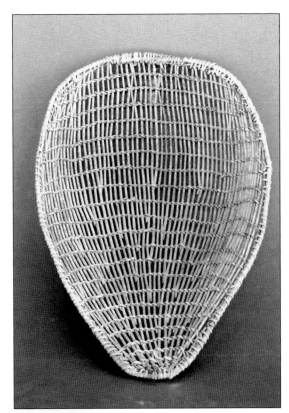

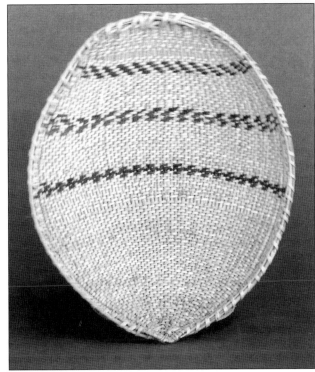

Tightly woven baskets were used to roast pine nuts. Hot charcoals were continuously tossed and shaken to mix with and heat the seeds.

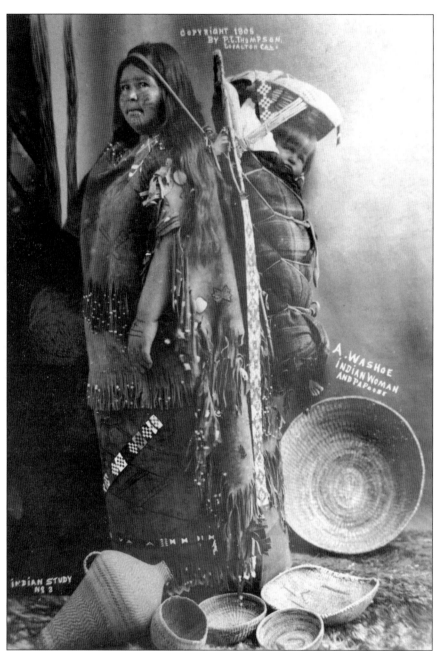

An unidentified Washo woman with her baby in a cradleboard, *c.* 1905, wears a buckskin dress and stands amid willow baskets. Washo women were valued for their energy and self-effacing manner, as well as generosity and the ability to endure hunger and discomfort. Looking closely at her face, we notice Washo ceremonial paint, used on special occasions. It was made from earth within tribal lands, or traded from other tribes. Decorations on her dress might include shell beads, valued because they were carried from the Pacific Ocean. The coiled cooking baskets, made of white willow, were so tightly woven that they would hold water brought to a boil by dropping in heated stones. Created from willows and twigs collected in late summer, they were made during the winter when the men chipped arrowheads and made hunting weapons and tools.

Washo cradleboards differed in design for female and male infants. The female version, seen here, features a zigzag design on the sunshade, not visible here.

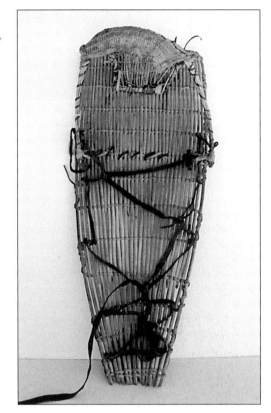

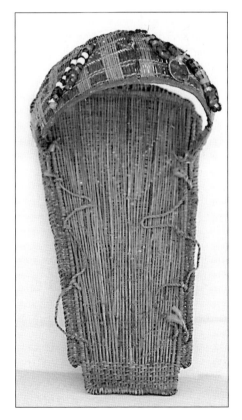

The male cradleboard was decorated by a series of diagonal parallel lines. Pendants of shell or part of the baby's umbilical cord were sometimes dangled from the removable sunshade.

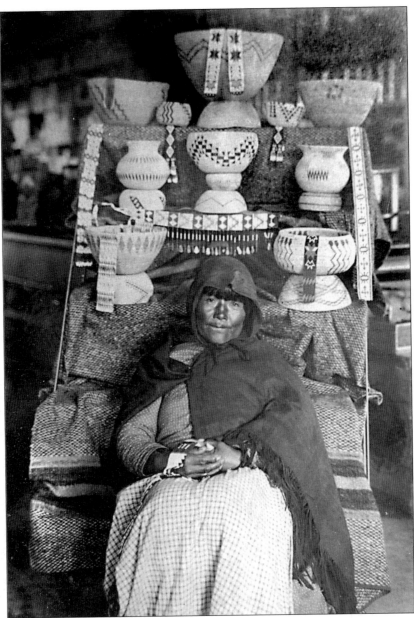

An unidentified Washo woman sits before a display of baskets. When Euro-American immigrants settled Washo lands, each of their activities—farming, ranching, mining, lumbering, and commercial fishing—altered the environment and adversely affected Washo life. The animals the Indians hunted migrated out of Washo territory; gathering lands were fenced for domestic animals to graze; fishing at Lake Tahoe was reserved for whites; rivers were diverted for irrigation and poisoned by mining chemicals; forests were clear-cut. As Washo men found work as ranch hands or laborers, the women began to make decorative baskets for sale, rather than the utilitarian baskets of earlier times. By the early 1900's Washo women were acknowledged as being among the finest basket makers in the world. Here an unidentified woman sits before an exhibit of baskets, the largest of which may have taken months to weave. Each of the pieces earned her food or clothing in trade, or a small amount of money.

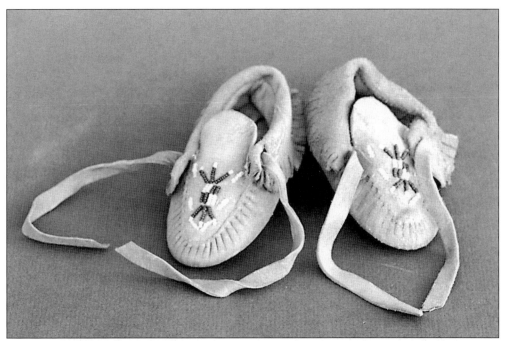

The artistry and craftsmanship of the Washo are shown here in a pair of buckskin moccasins with beaded design on the top, made for a child.

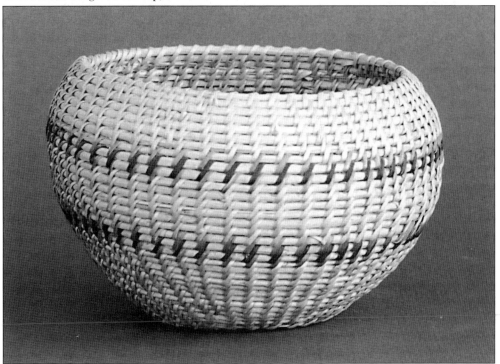

Patience and attention to detail define the art of California Native American basketry. Like other native basketmakers, Washo artisans can often be identified by their distinctive designs, and by the ticking of a colored band of fiber woven into the rim.

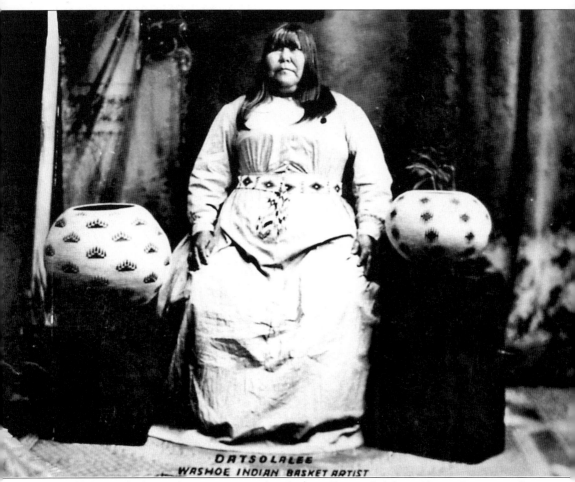

DATSOLALEE
WASHOE INDIAN BASKET ARTIST

World-famous basket maker Dat So La Li lived parts of her early life in Alpine County, washing and cooking for miners at Silver Mountain. Her given name was Da bu da, which means "young willow," coincidentally the material she later used in her woven masterpieces. Her work became known universally for its shapes, weave, and symbolic designs. Her delicacy of touch, artistic skill, and poetic imagery was unsurpassed. She produced as many as 30 stitches to the inch from splits in the willow made using her fingernails and teeth. By 1903, her baskets brought unheard-of prices from collectors, ranging from $150 to well over $250. Today her work is deemed priceless.

By the end of the 19th century, Native Americans began making their crafts for the marketplace. These items were "made for sale," and were marketed by reservation trading posts or to travelers along the new highway systems.

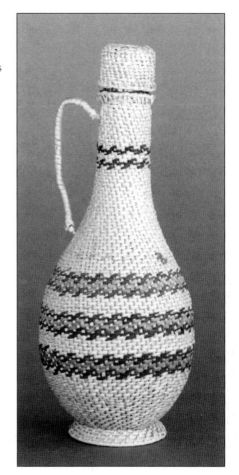

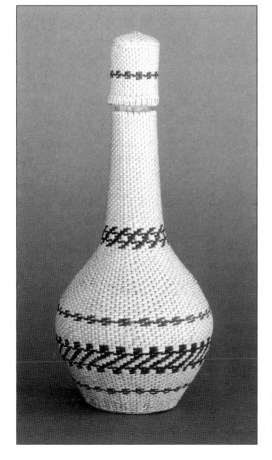

Willow-covered bottles are good examples of Washo craft adapted to Euro-American material culture. Bracken fern stitches, juxtaposed with those of willow, created rows of dark and light patterns.

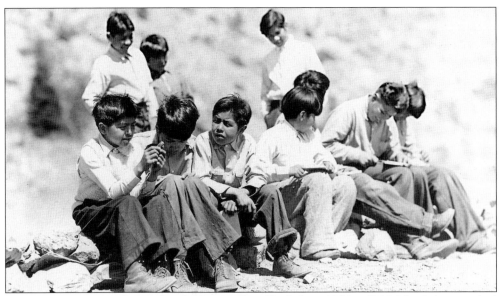

Leonore M. Bravo taught Washo children in Woodfords from 1937 to 1939. The fathers worked for the road department or as hands on local ranches. The school was segregated, partly because Indian children had contracted trachoma, a highly contagious eye disease, and there was fear of it spreading to non-Indians. During those years, the opportunity to develop better understanding between races was missed, but the Washo gained a good education. Bravo commented that "the school was a very happy place to be. There was never such a thing as a discipline problem. The children were quiet, studied, and learned well."

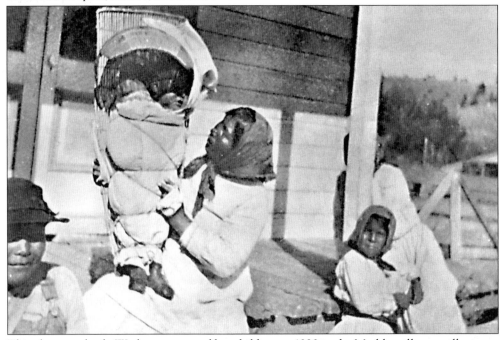

This photograph of a Washo woman and her children, c. 1920 in the Markleeville area, illustrates the mix of Washo tradition and acculturation. The house is a wooden structure, modern for its day, yet she still utilizes the traditional cradleboard.

Reginald George, pictured here, was a student at the Woodfords School in 1938.

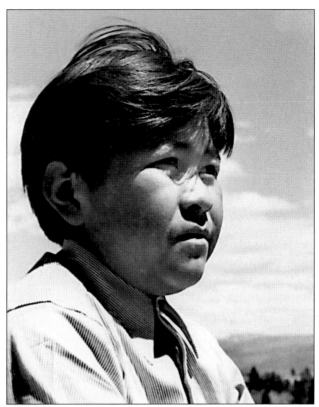

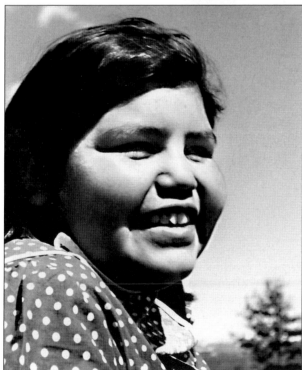

Teola Sally, pictured here, was also a student at the Woodfords School in 1938. Reginald and Teola's families, like all Native Americans, were bound by an 1890s law stipulating that they must have non-Indian surnames in order to receive land allotments—in the case of the Washo, Anglo first names, issued by a United States agent seeking to acculturate the tribes.

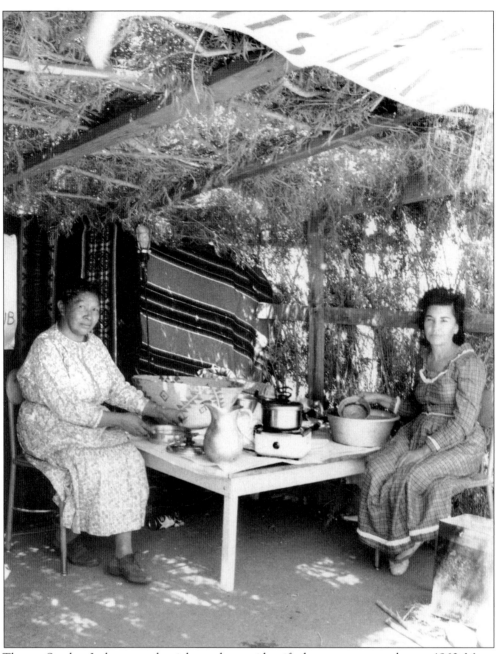

Theresa Smokey Jackson, on the right, and an unidentified woman are seen here c. 1960. Many Washo living in urban America have attempted to maintain their culture and traditions. In 1970, the 80-acre Hung-a-lel-ti "colony" was established in Woodfords, providing the Washo with their first tribal land in Alpine County since the 19th century.

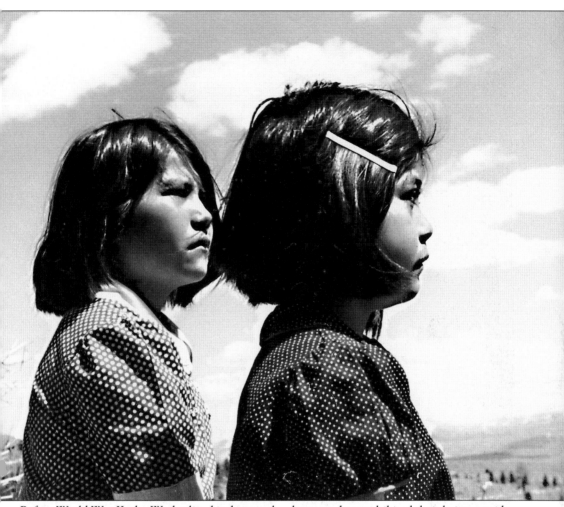

Before World War II, the Washo lived indoors only when weather prohibited their being outside. Latter-day Washo winter homes were generally one-room cabins, sometimes divided into sleeping quarters and a living/cooking room. Inside the cabins, they used tables, chairs, beds, and an assortment of utensils for cooking and eating. Outdoors they normally used their traditional tools. Washo children were bilingual. Their teacher, Leonore Bravo, commented, "Their language was soft and beautiful, and whether they spoke Washo or English, it came out in poetic form."

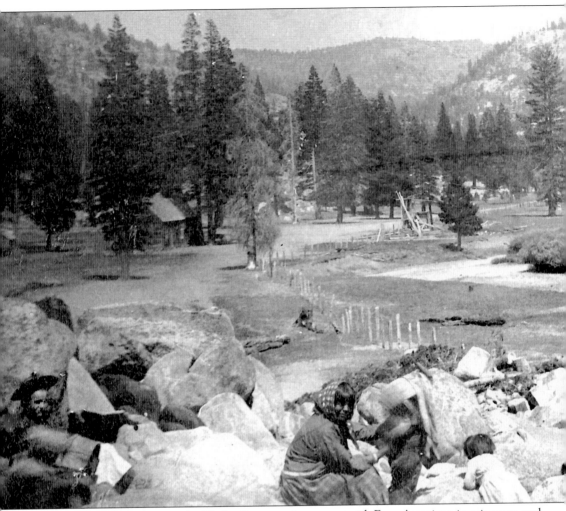

It has been 175 years since the Washo first came in contact with Euro-American immigrants, and they are continuing their struggle to recreate a homeland. In the early 1980s, the tribe created the Washo Cultural Foundation, which strives to secure land at Lake Tahoe, and renew traditional language and education. In 1988, the tribe won a competitive bid for a 20-year lease to act as proprietor of Lake Tahoe's Meeks Bay Resort. They are currently fighting to protect one of their most sacred sites, Lake Tahoe's De-ek Wadapush, also known as Cave Rock. An unidentified Washo woman and her children are pictured here in Hermit Valley in 1880.

Two

Mining Towns
and Camps

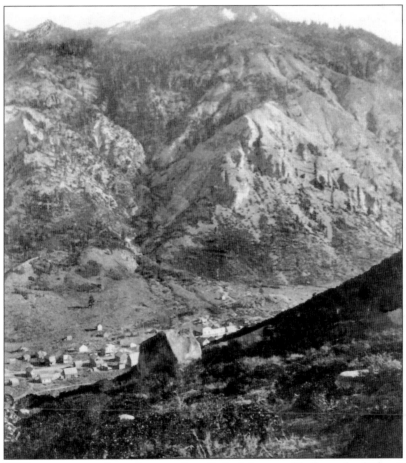

In this c. 1867 view, a stereopticon photographer climbed the steep bluffs north of Silver Mountain to capture this view, looking south at the town site. In its heyday, Silver Mountain is estimated to have had as many as 3,500 inhabitants, nearly all of them fevered silver seekers.

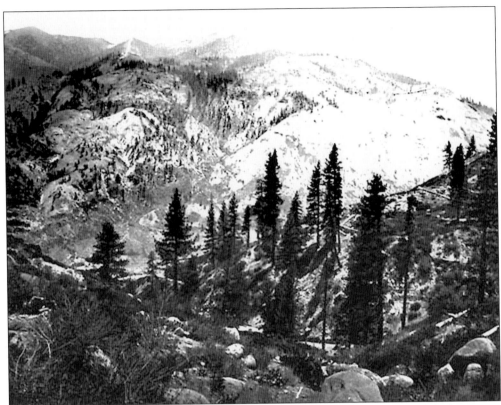

Once heavily forested, Silver Mountain and its environs were soon largely denuded of trees.

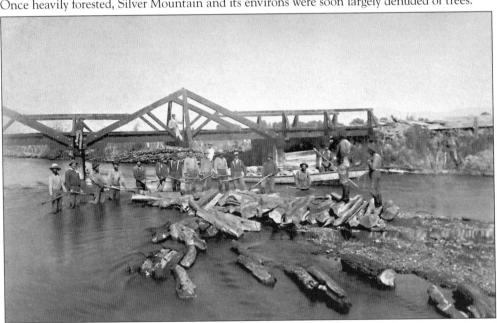

Timber was used both near and far. After local construction needs were filled, timber was floated down the Carson River to Empire, Nevada, to build the Comstock mineshafts and mills and to feed their boilers.

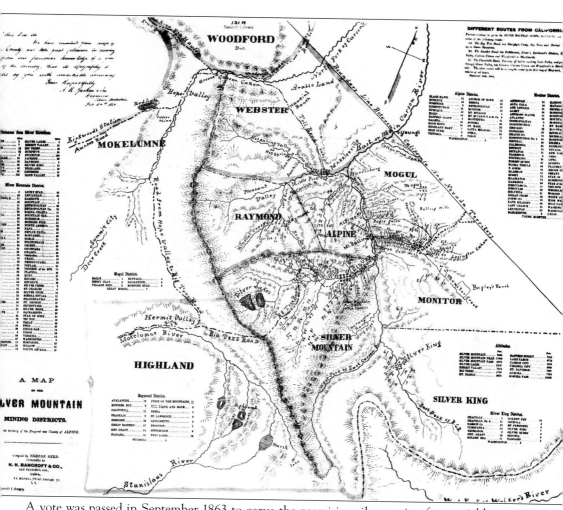

A vote was passed in September 1863 to carve the promising silver region from neighboring counties. The following March, newly minted Alpine County selected Silver Mountain as its county seat. Here an 1864 map shows the Silver Mountain mining districts.

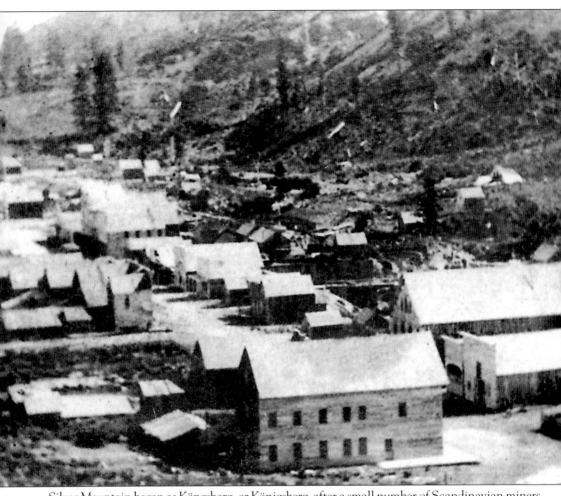

Silver Mountain began as Köngsberg, or Königsberg, after a small number of Scandinavian miners began prospecting at the headwaters of Silver Creek in the fall of 1860. By some accounts, they arrived as early as 1858. However, the first major discovery, which turned out to be the mountain ledge, was made by three other prospectors, variously identified as John Johnson, Wesley Poole (or Perry), and V. Harrison (or Harris). These three men reportedly returned to Virginia City, Nevada, after spending three days in the Scandinavian Canyon area. But they soon returned with an expanded party of prospectors to work the Scandinavian and Mountain leads. By 1862, some 2,000 men swarmed the area, encouraged by reports such as that of the *Mining and Scientific Press*: "The Mountain ledge and mountain ranks A No. 1. The rock was something similar to that of the Ophir and Virginia City. I have seen the assays of it $672.10 and $860.73 silver per ton." But the ore did not live up to expectations, and slowly the town's stature diminished. Silver Mountain lost the county government to Markleeville in 1875—although it retained the distinction of having the only jail in the territory. In 1878, news of a silver strike in Bodie, 70 miles away in Nevada, was an irresistible draw for the miners who had hung on. With the exodus of residents, businesses closed and relocated to more prosperous areas. The county newspaper, the *Alpine Chronicle*, finally abandoned its dwindling readership, having published a farewell acknowledging the mining industry's demise and the transformation of Silver Mountain into a ghost town.

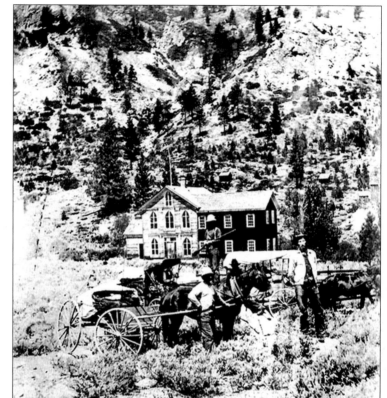

The Isabella boarding house, built *c.* 1870 to provide housing for miners, served for many years as a well-known landmark on what is now Highway 4. By 1929 however, the boarding house windows, as seen below, were gone, along with the bright promise of the once-bustling silver mines.

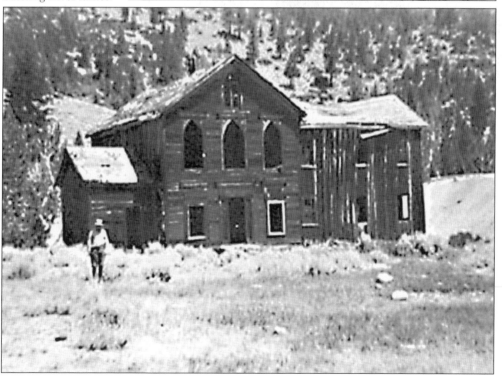

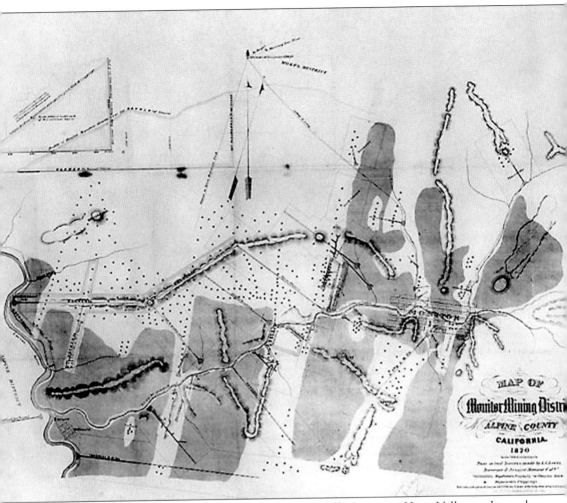

The first mine in Alpine County belonged to Uncle Billy Rogers in Hope Valley, and was also the first copper mine in California. Rancher L. L. Hawkins claimed to have discovered ore on Monitor Creek in 1857, and prospectors roamed over Silver Mountain during the summer of 1858. But it was not until June 1861, that men named Johnson, Harris, and Perry discovered and located claims known as Mountain No. 1 and Silver Creek on Silver Mountain. By 1864, there were 200 claims in 10 mining districts in Alpine County. In 1866 the number had grown to between 300 and 400 claims in 14 districts. Most ledges were abandoned within a year or two. Two mines that proved valuable, the Tarshish and the Advance, were the major producers in the Monitor District. The town of Monitor unsuccessfully vied with neighboring Silver Mountain to be the county seat. While the mines of Monitor were both more prosperous and longer-lived than those of Silver Mountain, by 1876 the commotion had died down. The bonanzas dreamed of when this map of Monitor was drawn, never materialized. (Courtesy of the California State Library Collection..)

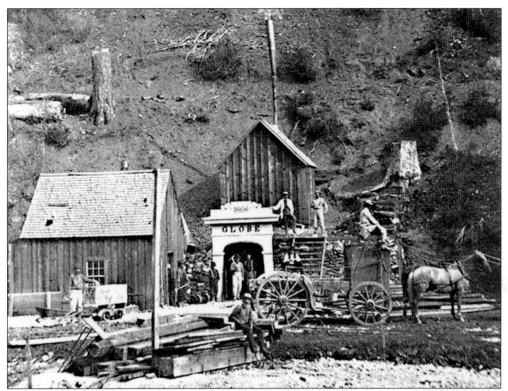

The Globe Gold & Silver Mining Company, one of the biggest mining operations in Monitor Canyon, was incorporated in 1863. Its most famous lode, the Tarshish, produced a variety of rich specimens, inducing investors to lavish substantial sums on a double-tracked tunnel, a 10- to 15-horsepower engine, and a four-inch Cornish pump. (Courtesy of the California State Library Collection.)

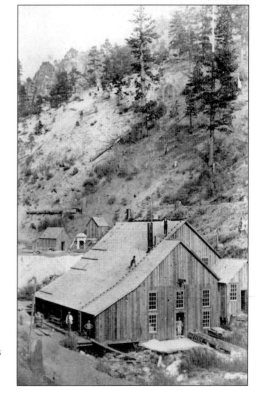

A 58-by-61-foot mill was erected at the Globe Mine in 1871. But like other local mines, the Globe's ore proved unprofitable, and operations ceased about 1873. (Courtesy of the California State Library Collection.)

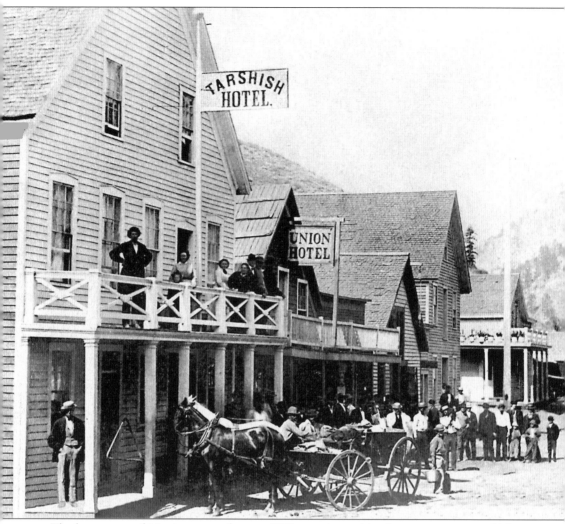

The boomtown of Monitor, seen above c. 1870, was situated in the narrow canyon of Monitor Creek. Its lone street, composed of 600 lots, stretched a mile in length. The inhabitants graded the slopes and filled in the creek to increase construction sites, but their efforts left Monitor bereft of flowing water. At its rowdy zenith, over 60 ledges were being mined, and it boasted fine hotels and first-class saloons. Only two years after it was founded, in 1863, the tumult generated by discoveries in the area began to subside. The people who had rushed in did not have the money required to develop their claims. A sullen calm settled over the area until April 1867, when a rich vein of ore, discovered in the Tarshish mine, regenerated the excitement. The 7,100 pounds of ore paid $400 a ton "making it the richest mine on the Pacific coast, if not in the world." A new era had dawned. The merriment halted briefly in April 1872, when fire destroyed a large section of the commercial district. Within days, enterprising businessmen were rebuilding. (Courtesy of the California State Library Collection.)

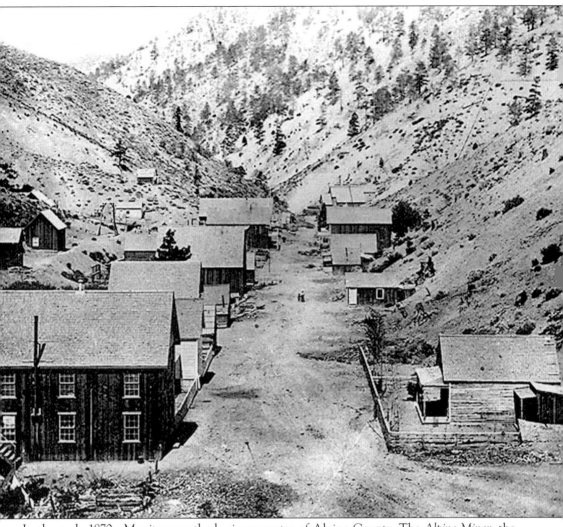

In the early 1870s, Monitor was the business center of Alpine County. The *Alpine Miner,* the town's newspaper, crowed, "From Monitor flows the money into the hands of miners and others employed in prosecuting mining enterprises, and to Monitor come the farmers of Carson, Diamond, Antelope and Slinkard valleys with their produce." In 1871, there were six saloons in town and two more being built. There were no idle men living there, and the paper was advertising for more good workers. By 1873, the mines had again fallen on hard times, and the paltry returns caused the town's population to gradually dwindle. In 1880, Monitor's population stood at 200, and the town would never regain its former stature. In 1888, the town was renamed "Loope," after a prominent local doctor. This photograph shows Monitor in 1872. (Courtesy of the California State Library Collection.)

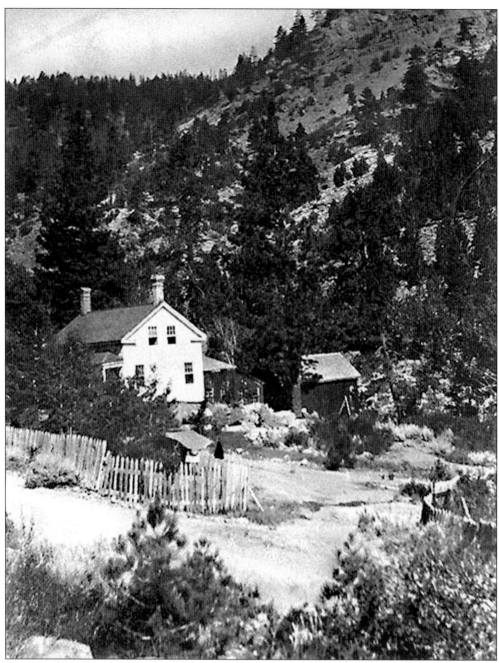

Lewis Chalmers came to Alpine County at the end of 1866 to oversee British interests in the local silver mines. Running mines and mills was sometimes overwhelming for the "English Gentleman." Lewis once wrote that "angry miners had attacked the pigs and chickens of the mine foreman and killed all of the animals over a wage dispute." Chalmers acquired Daniel Davidson's cabin and sawmill in 1876. He soon enlarged the modest home and furnished it lavishly—leading townsfolk to call it "Chalmers' Mansion." Chalmers's fortunes in the silver business rose and fell until 1885. When the mines shut down, he left his wife and children and returned to England to try to find funds to pay a mountain of debt. The photograph above was taken c. 1915.

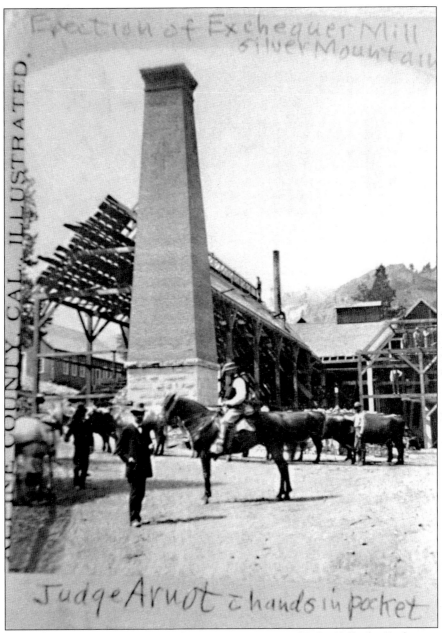

Erection of Exchequer Mill
Silver Mountain

ALPINE COUNTY, CAL. ILLUSTRATED.

Judge Arnot c hands in pocket

Here the Exchequer Quartz Mill is under construction, *c.* 1872. In 1869, the Exchequer Gold and Silver Mining Company was formed in London with Lewis Chalmers as its United States agent. The company took over two mines at the head of Scandinavian Canyon and built the mill three years later. Two other British companies operated in the district at the same time supplying needed capital to the county. Although at least one of the companies intermittently worked up to three shifts in one of the mines, in the early 1870's there were indications of mismanagement in all three, and no evidence that the ledges sought were ever hit. Chalmers continued his mining activities for 19 years, but failed to earn enough wealth to sustain himself and his family. Alpine County judge N. D. Arnot (in the photograph with hands in his pockets) eventually foreclosed on this and many of Chalmers' properties.

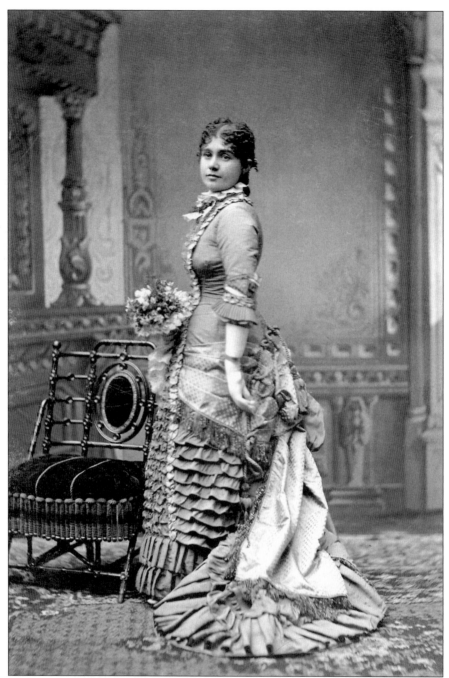

Lovely widow Antoinette Laughton, with a son in tow, first made her Alpine County appearance as housekeeper for London capitalist Lewis Chalmers in 1876. By the end of 1880, Mrs. Laughton was Chalmers's wife. At her wedding in San Francisco's Grace Cathedral, she wore an elaborate gown the color of "ashes of roses." The marriage was fodder for local gossip for years. It was believed that "Lady Chalmers" was not a widow, but had had her son out of wedlock. It was further rumored that Chalmers had abandoned a wife in England. The marriage between Antoinette and "Captain" Chalmers lasted a number of years, but was tempestuous and eventually ended in tragedy.

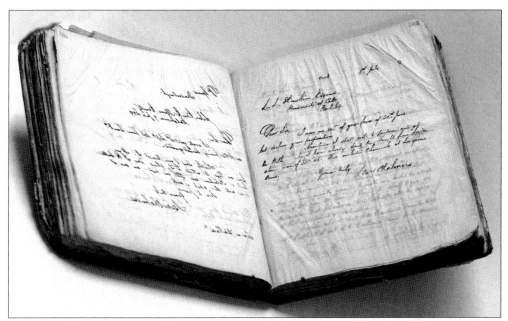

Antoinette's husband, Lewis Chalmers, departed for England in 1885, ostensibly to raise funds for his silver-mining enterprises. Though he continued to correspond with his wife for years, Chalmers never returned to Silver Mountain. He died in London in 1904 in what the Aberdeen newspaper delicately called "comparative obscurity." The 19th-century writings of Lewis Chalmers are found in over 5000 pages of his business and personal correspondence saved for posterity in the books shown here.

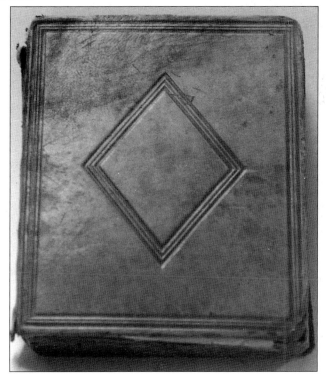

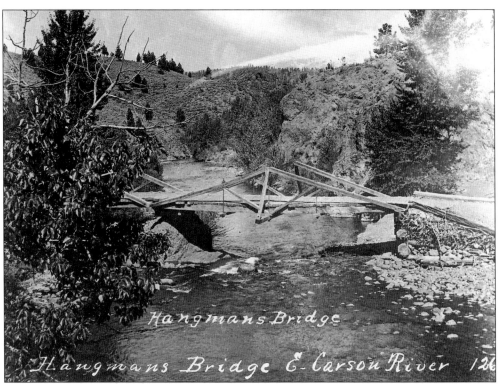

Hangmans Bridge

Hangmans Bridge E. Carson River 126

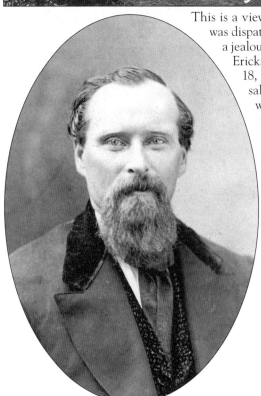

This is a view of Hangman's Bridge, where Ernst Reusch was dispatched by vigilantes on April 17, 1874. Reusch, a jealous husband, shot E. H. Erickson, seen at left, at Erickson's saloon in Silver Mountain on December 18, 1872. The murder weapon had been left in the saloon by a notorious character, Charles P. Goff, who was at that time the county judge. After many months trying, unsuccessfully, to find an unbiased jury, county officials decided to transfer Reusch to Mono County for a fair trial. A group of armed men dispensed their own brand of summary justice on the bridge.

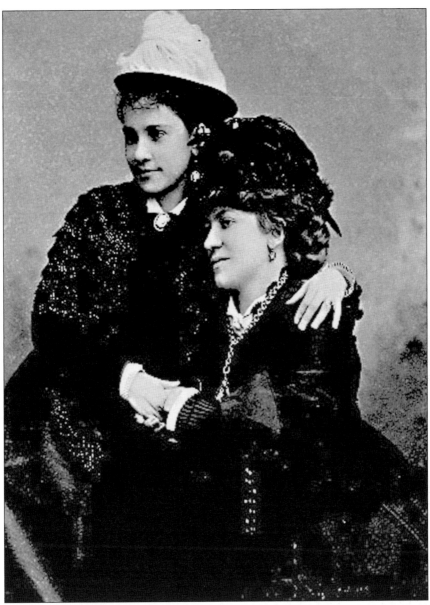

By the 1880s, women had begun to express themselves in more than just their choice of finery. Pioneering voices also began to call for the right to vote, a struggle that did not succeed until 1920, when the 19th Amendment was ratified. Women began to hold elected offices early in Alpine County history. Several women held the post of county school superintendent before the turn of the century—the first being Anna Spencer in 1877. Elizabeth Ellis Coyan held the office of county tax collector and treasurer for an incredible 49 years. When first seeking office in 1919, she campaigned on horseback, a practice long abandoned by the time her career ended in 1968. Another interesting figure to serve as a county official was Lucille Brown, the first female to be appointed county sheriff in California. She had worked undercover on at least one case for her husband, who was the sheriff until his death in an automobile accident in 1957. She succeeded him, completing his term in 1958. This portrait shows a Miss Harrison and Miss Milton at Silver Mountain, c. 1881.

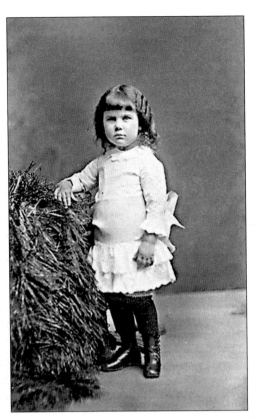

Poor Raymond H. Arnot, son of N. D. Arnot, was forced to endure a common practice in the 19th century—being outfitted in a dress for a formal portrait.

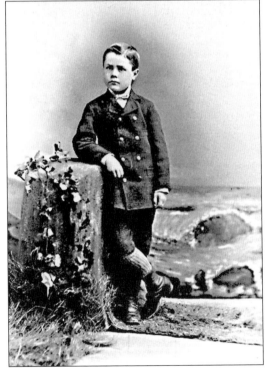

Little boys looked forward to the day they were allowed to graduate to long trousers. Young Arnot poses in knickers for this studio portrait, taken in San Francisco c. 1881. Raymond was one of at least ten children of N. D. Arnot, a judge in Alpine County from 1880 to 1904.

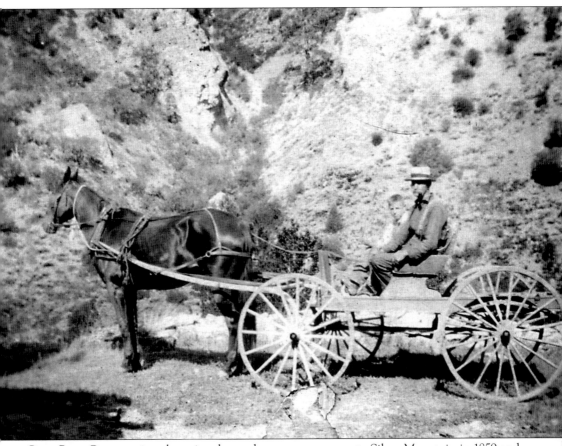

Capt. Peter Curtz, posing above in a horse-drawn wagon, came to Silver Mountain in 1859 and made several fortunes mining and milling. Besides a prosperous lifelong mining career—in 1915 he owned and managed some 22 claims in the Mogul District alone—Captain Curtz, as his friends called him, served as Alpine County district attorney, county supervisor ,and school board member. Curtz Lake, 2.5 miles north of Markleeville, is named for him.

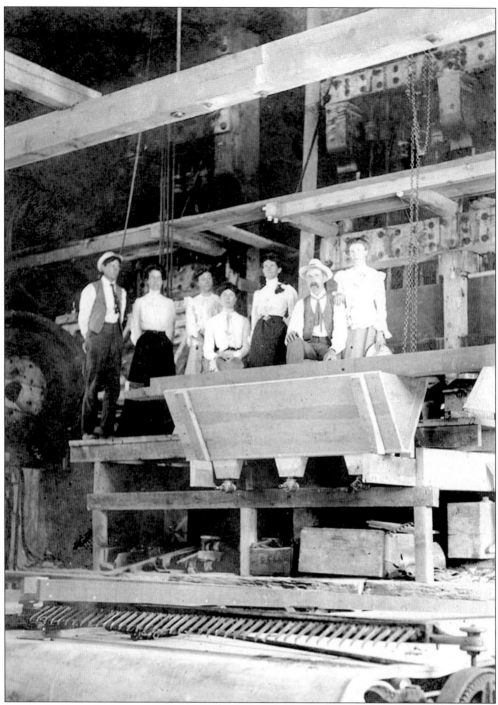

Inside the Curtz Mill, raw silver ore was crushed into a fine powdery texture by iron battery stamps. The crushed ore, called fines, was then shipped to the smelter for the extraction of valuable silver from the rock matrix. This Curtz family photograph must have been taken on a day when the mill was shut down, as the sound of iron stamps crushing the ore would have been deafening to visitors.

Three

EARLY SETTLEMENTS

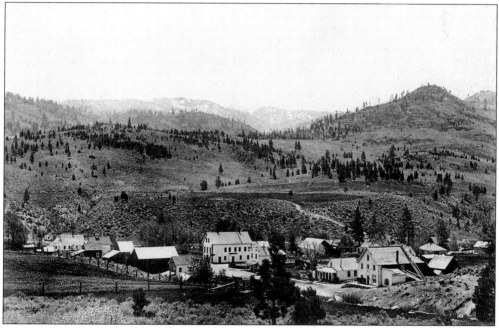

In the 1850s, both the Utah Territory and the new state of California claimed the land that is now Alpine County. In August of 1855, surveyor George Henry Goddard found it to be part of California. In 1864, a county was created from sections of neighboring counties and was given the name Alpine, "for it will be one of the highest counties on the continent." The new county reached its peak in population, an estimated 5,000, when it was created. As mines failed, the population dwindled, and although some mining continued and the cattle, sheep, and the timber industries prospered, much of the area remained wilderness. On March 8, 1867, a gray wolf trotted down the main street of the county seat, Silver Mountain, causing great excitement. To this day, similar enthusiasm is generated when a bear roams the streets of Markleeville or gathers apples from the trees in Woodfords.

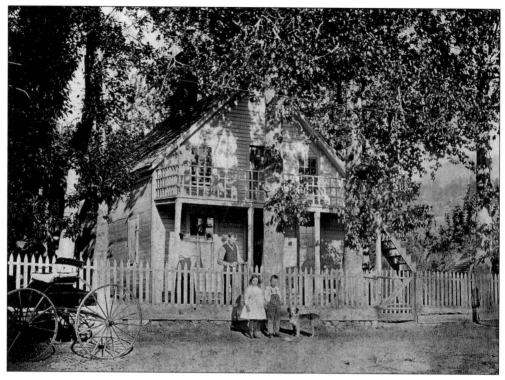

In the 1860s, six or seven homesteading families settled in an Alpine County valley named for its shape, Diamond Valley. They established several sawmills and ranches, utilizing the flat grasslands to graze cattle. Pictured above is Mary Hawkin's Diamond Valley home, *c.* 1885. One of the valley's most famous residents was John A. "Snowshoe" Thompson, who superintended mines, built roads, and hauled goods and mail across the Sierra. Thompson and Washo Indians constructed the first irrigation ditches in the eastern Sierra to bring water from the West Carson River to Diamond Valley. Water was as precious as the minerals in Alpine County, a fact emphasized by pioneer descendent Gary Coyan, who remembers his grandfather carrying his shotgun when he went to irrigate. Descendents of three of the families that homesteaded Diamond Valley, the Coyans, the Barbers, and the Hawkins, still live in Alpine County.

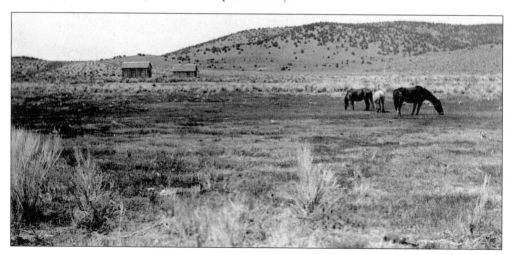

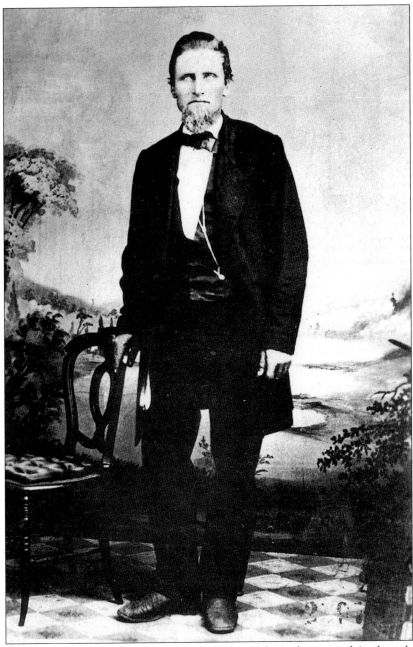

Diamond Valley settler John A. Tostensen is better known by his nickname and Anglicized surname, Snowshoe Thompson. For 20 years, he traversed the Sierra in winter on oak skis that he crafted himself, and for nine of those years he carried mail on his back. His treks opened the most direct route between the eastern Sierra and central California. In February 1859, a correspondent for a California newspaper, noting Thompson's ability to persevere in the extreme cold and storms of the Sierra, commented that he "must have been born either on or under a snow drift." Thompson's description of his skis was published in the *Alpine Chronicle* in 1869: nine feet long, turned up in front and flat bottomed; four inches wide in front, three inches behind, and one inch thick in the center. (Courtesy of the Nevada Historical Society.)

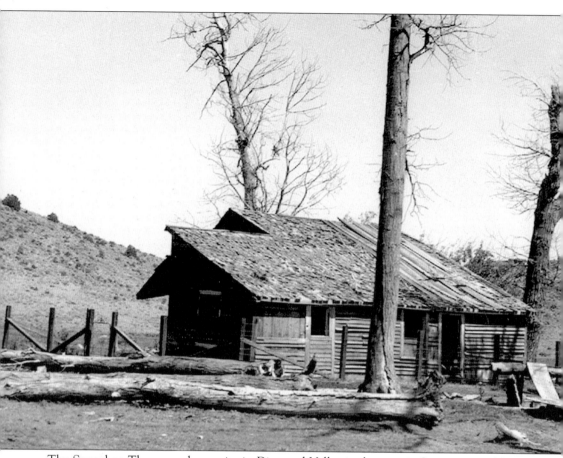

The Snowshoe Thompson home site in Diamond Valley is close to six Sierra passes: Monitor, Ebbetts, Carson, Luther, Echo, and Daggett (Kingsbury Grade). He traversed all of them in winter, carrying mail over Ebbetts to the town of Murphy's, and over Carson or Luther and Echo to Placerville. His treks took between two and four days during which he ate jerky and hardtack and slept under whatever shelter rocks or trees could provide.

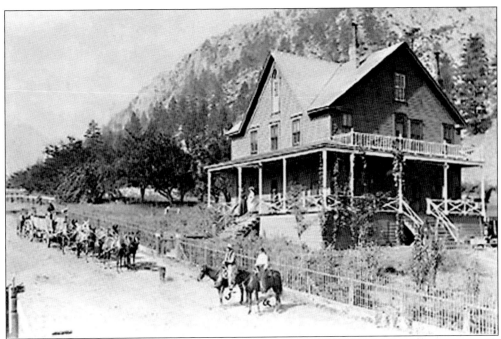

In 1847, a Mormon outpost called Brannon Springs was established at what later became the junction of Carson Canyon and Markleeville Roads. In 1853, when John Cary erected a water-powered sawmill and, later, a flour and gristmill near the site, the name became Cary's Mills. But in 1849, Daniel Woodford had built a hotel on the river, across the emigrant trail, and in 1869, when a post office was established there, the camp was officially named Woodfords. This photograph shows the Woodfords Hotel in 1902.

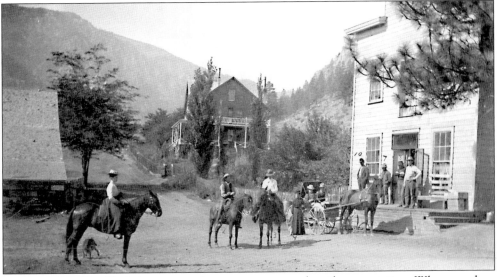

In the 1860s, Woodfords became an important stage and mail-route station. When ranches, farms, and mining towns developed around the camp, it became the transportation hub of Alpine County. In 1867, when Capt. D. A. Nye built a hall with a "fine spring floor" for dancing, it became "a favorite place of resort." The hall may be the building in back when this photograph was taken in 1902.

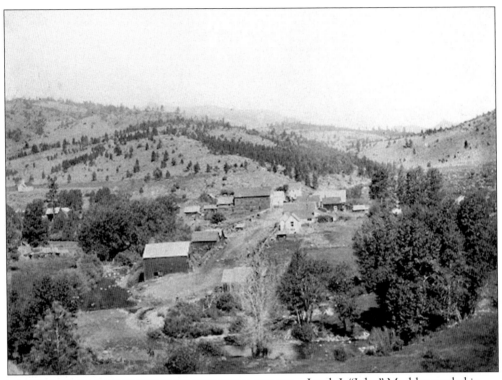

Jacob J. "John" Marklee settled in the place later named Markleeville in September 1861. By August 1863, 50 families lived there, and by the following year, illustrating what one visitor called "Yankee-go-aheaded-ness," the growing population expanded the town. Unlike those to the city of Silver Mountain and other mountain townships, the roads to Markleeville could be maintained almost year-round. The town had the usual assortment of businesses and professionals for a Western mining town, including eight lawyers, six hurdy-gurdy girls, and one much-needed minister.

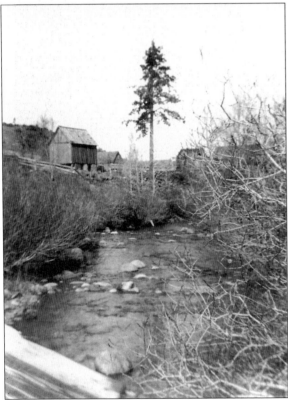

Early in the 20th century, thick-walled buildings were used as icehouses in Markleeville. Blocks of ice were cut from the river and stacked, and sides of beef or pigs were stored there. Sawdust placed between the blocks ensured that the ice lasted through the summer.

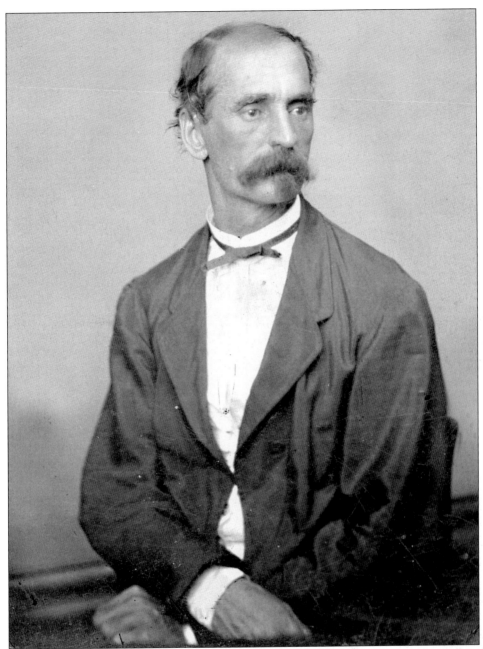

The first killing in the area occurred when Jacob Marklee, pictured here, was shot to death by H. W. Tuttle. On June 23, 1862, Marklee recorded a land claim of 160 acres that became the Markleeville town site. Marklee established and maintained a toll station, collecting fees from travelers when their cargo and livestock crossed the Middle Fork of the Carson River. Although toll station operators were always unpopular, and at least one other collector was shot in that era, Marklee was not killed by an irate traveler. Marklee had "benefited and befriended" Tuttle, who later killed him in an argument over property rights. A year later, Tuttle was acquitted of murder in Amador County District Court, when he was found to have acted in self defense. Marklee's home site was located where the Markleeville courthouse now stands.

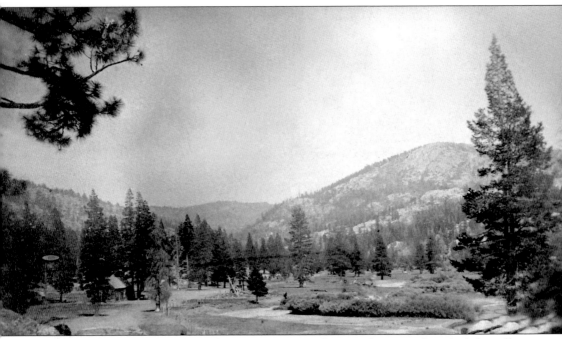

Hermit Valley is 12 miles from Silver Mountain. One historical account described the valley as "situated at the western foot of the eastern summit, on the north side of the south fork of the Mokelumne River." When Snowshoe Thompson carried mail between Genoa and Murphy's Camp, he traveled by way of Hermit Valley, where he often stayed the night in some abandoned cabin. On some trips the snow was so deep he needed to use his balance pole to find the rooftop. Then he would tear boards from the gable end and drop inside.

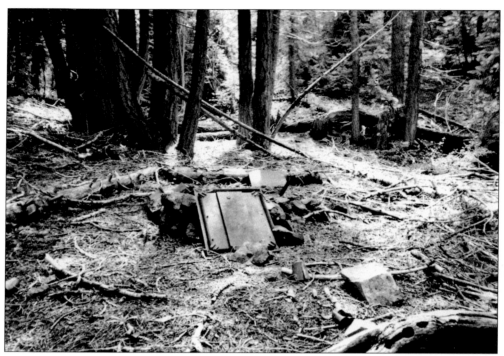

Raymond was a small settlement halfway between Silver Mountain and Markleeville. The town's drugstore and saloon sites have provided collectors with bottles and artifacts over the years. Legend says that because the owners planned to return, the whiskey from the saloon was stored in barrels and hidden in a tunnel, the mouth of which was filled in. Regarding that legendary buried treasure, Harry Hawkins commented in 1967, "It sure would be aged!"

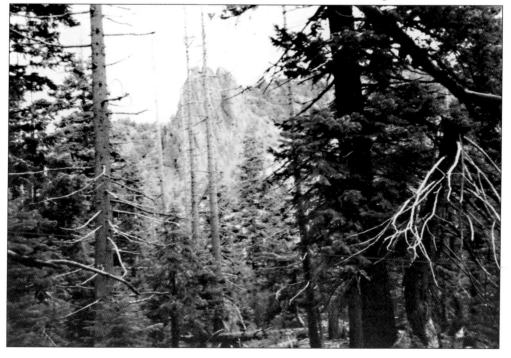

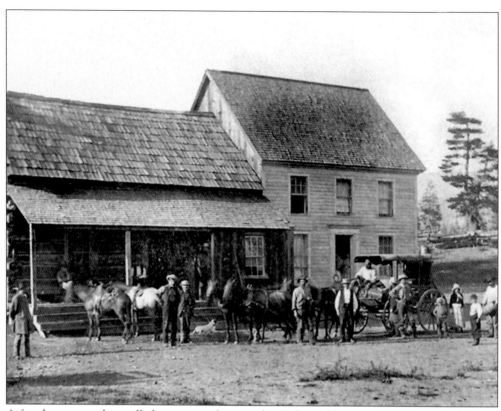

A four-horse team has pulled a stagecoach up to the Kirkwood Inn way station, across the road from the Kirkwood Meadows. The site lies at the junction of three counties. By walking around the building you have traveled from Alpine County to El Dorado and Amador Counties.

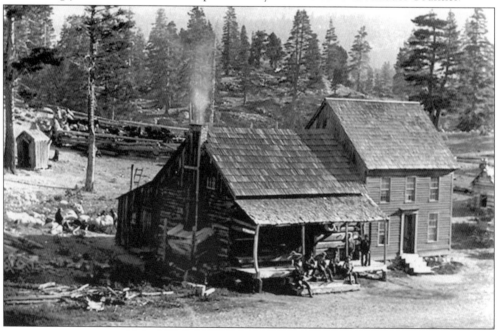

Col. William "Uncle Billy" Rogers was a local legend in the eastern Sierra in the 1850s and 1860s. Formerly a frontiersman, scout, and sheriff of El Dorado County, in the 1850s he developed a copper mine that operated in Hope Valley for more than 30 years. In 1859, unable to prevent the hanging of his friend Lucky Bill Thorington, he left the area for the Ruby Mountains in Nevada, where he settled on the Shoshone Indian reservation. This gold pan, in the Alpine County Museum, is said to have been used by Rogers in county streams.

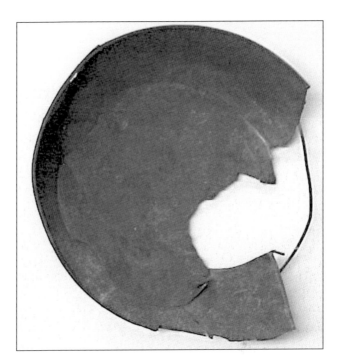

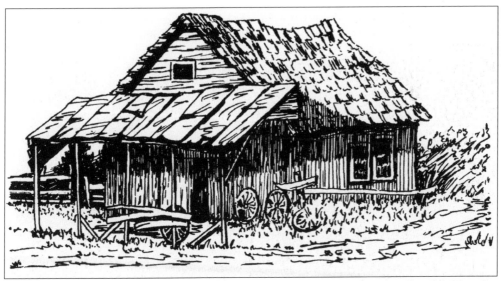

In 1852, 20-year-old John Studebaker established a blacksmith shop in Hope Valley, shown in this drawing by Dede Lyons. Previously, he had built wagons for the family firm in Indiana. Here he specialized as a wheelwright, repairing immigrants' wagons before their last push over the Sierra. In 1853, Studebaker moved to Placerville, where he manufactured wheelbarrows for the mines. Eventually he earned an $8,000 stake that he put back into the family business, and earned a fortune turning the firm into the Studebaker Automobile Company.

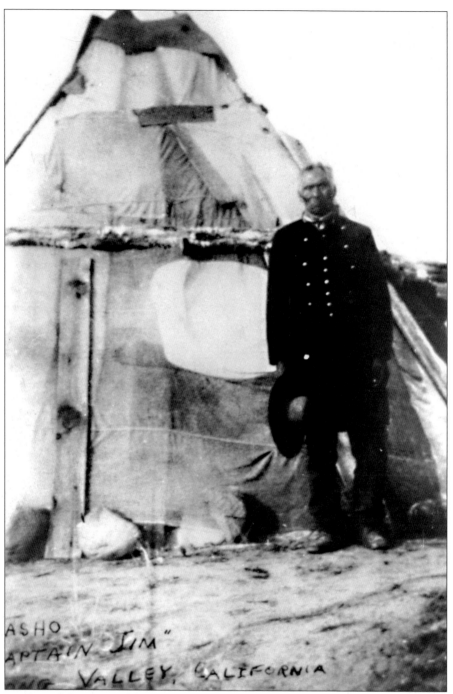

Captain Jim, of the Hung-a-lel-ti band, was the first of the Washo Indians to be recognized by whites as a tribal leader. He traveled to Sacramento and helped negotiate a price of $1.25 per acre for land taken by the immigrants. The legislature never approved the expenditure, and no money was ever paid. The name Captain Jim came to signify tribal leadership, and two others took the name afterwards. This photograph shows the first Captain Jim near the present-day Hung-a-lel-ti community.

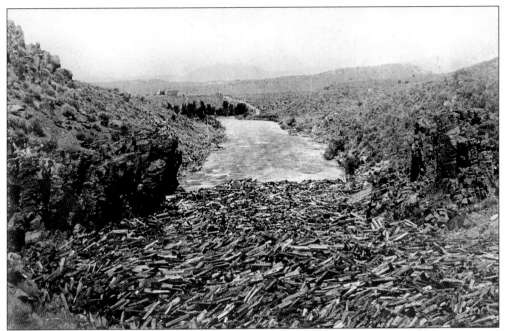

Between the years 1860 and 1882, millions of feet of sawn logs, mining timber, and cordwood ran down the Carson River. By 1864, there had been 14 sawmills built in the watershed, and in 1869, 13 logging companies engaged in cutting cordwood. Some of the wood was used locally, but much more sustained mining operations on Nevada's Comstock Lode. In 1866, it was estimated that 14 million board feet of lumber were transported on this river alone.

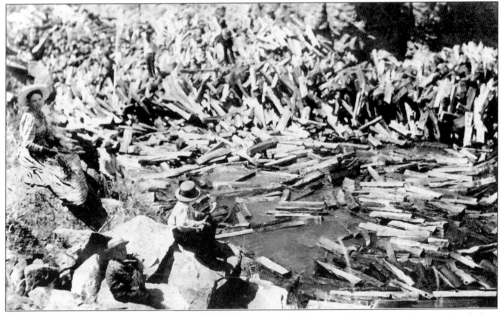

A log dam was built on a narrow part of the East Carson River, and the cut timber was hauled to the resulting lake. When it was filled to capacity, the dam was blown up, and the timber flowed down the Carson as far as Dayton, Nevada, where it was removed and hauled up the mountain to Virginia City.

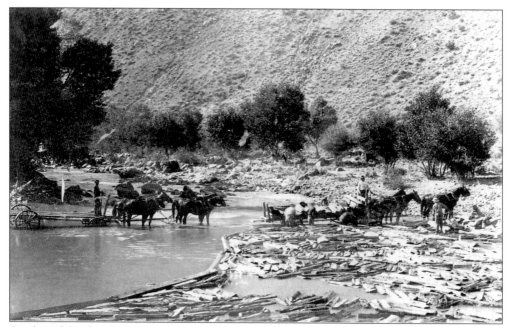

Cordwood for the Nevada mines was cut in the winter and stored until it was sent downstream in "drives" during spring freshets. Men stationed along the river prevented logjams with long, hooked poles. The cordwood took about 22 days to run from Alpine County to Empire, north of Carson City, Nevada, where it was removed and transported to Virginia City. There could be as many as six log drives in the Carson River during a spring season.

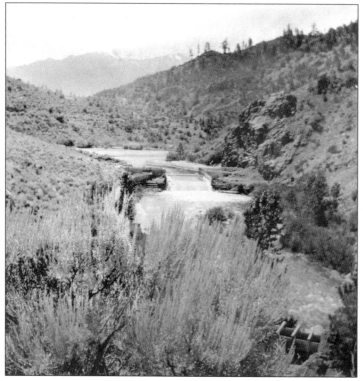

By the mid-1880s, one-fourth of Alpine County's forests had been removed. The denuding of the mountains caused abrupt spring thaws of snow packs that previously melted gradually. The result was floods in the spring, and dry riverbeds in the fall. Discussing the deforestation, the 1883 U.S. Geological Survey report stated, "The Sierra were devastated for a length of nearly 100 miles."

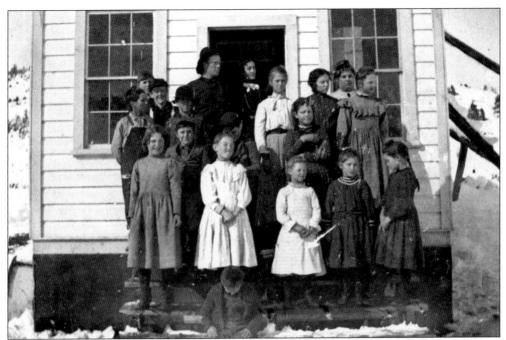

In August 1865, there were four school districts in Alpine County. The superintendent of schools earned an annual salary of $400; the four teachers (all men) were paid $69 a month. Pictured above is the class of 1900 on the porch steps of the Old Webster schoolhouse. The old Webster Schoolhouse is shown below in the 1960s, prior to community restoration. The restored schoolhouse is now listed on the National Register of Historic Places.

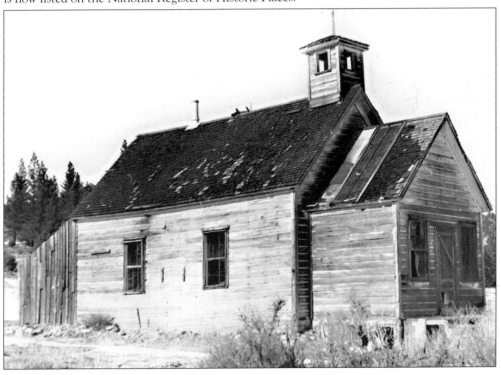

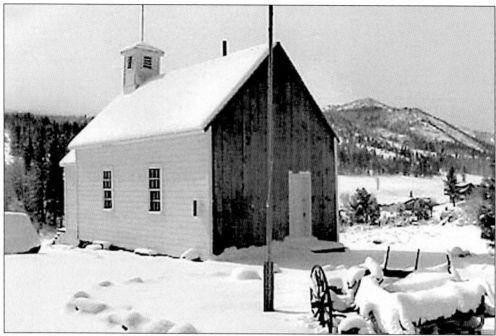

During the mining era, there were elementary schools in Fredericksburg, Diamond Valley, Markleeville, Monitor, and Silver Mountain. In 1867, there were 169 white children between 5 and 15 years old in Alpine County. As the mines faltered, the number of children dropped, so that by 1880 there were only 112, and in 1911 school attendance fell so low the county came close to losing state funding. The school board came up with a radical solution. While most schools east of the Sierra remained segregated, Alpine County began to encourage Indian children to attend. For the first time, due to the scarcity of white children, Washo children were provided an alternative to boarding at Stewart Indian School in Carson City, Nevada.

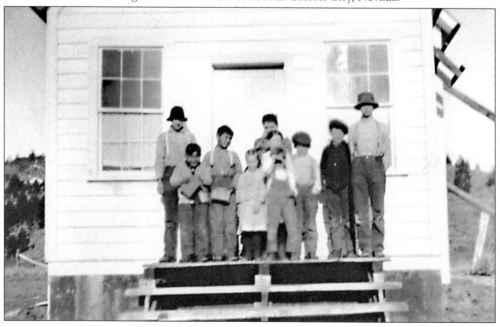

Louis Vallem was a cattle and sheep rancher in Long Valley who vowed not to marry his fiancée, Josephine Kenny, both pictured at right, until he saved $10,000. He succeeded in 1896 and moved the cash from the strong box under his sofa to the new bank in Minden, Nevada. The bank failed, and he lost everything. Meanwhile, Miss Kenny became a beloved teacher at Webster and Fredricksburg Schools in an era when a teacher who married was discharged because pregnancy might prevent her from working. So when Louis came courting, Miss Kenny's male students attempted to keep him away by pelting him with snowballs. Later she served as superintendent of schools. It was not until 1906 that Louis Vallem rebuilt his fortune and married Miss Kenny, by then 36 years old. She never recovered from bearing the last of four children at age 42, and died a few years later, in 1920.

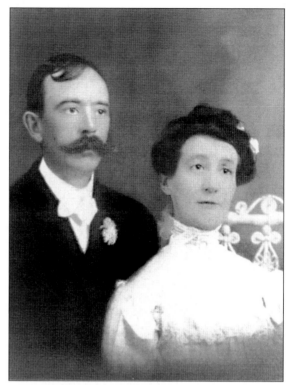

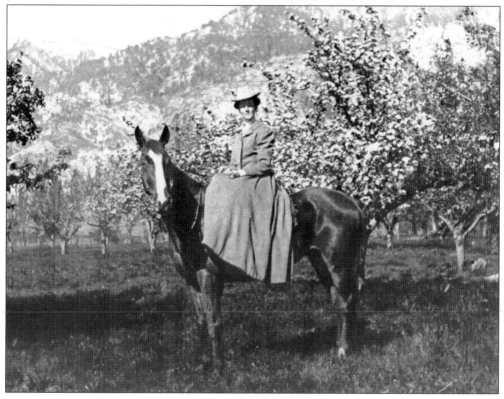

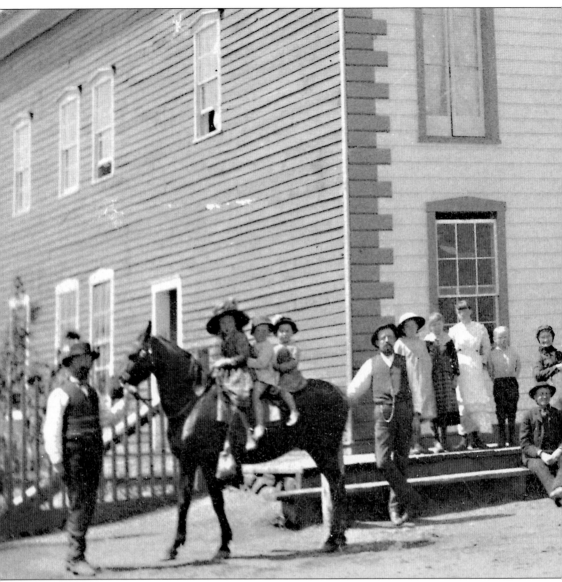

Judge Arnot is shown holding the bridle of a horse for three of his children in 1891. Arnot's oldest daughter was born in Silver Mountain, the others in Markleeville. Judge Arnot's wife, Anna, served a term as the county superintendent of schools, as had her father, Rev. R. H. Ford. The Arnots had five sons including Philip, who became a doctor, and John, who became a nationally known newspaper cartoonist. Rising 10,054 feet, Arnot Peak near Ebbetts Pass is named for Judge Arnot.

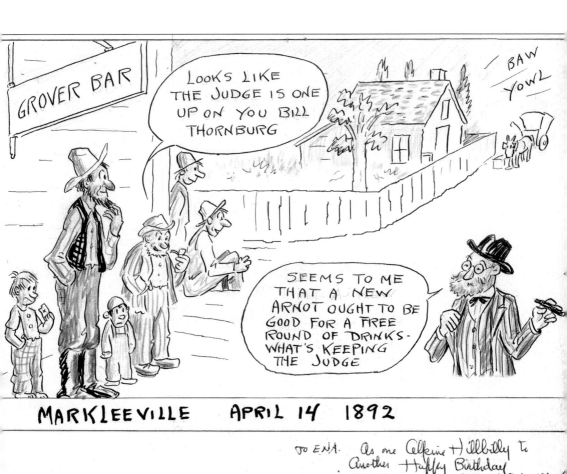

John P. Arnot, born in Markleeville, began his career as a cartoonist on San Francisco newspapers, and later became associated with the Eastman Kodak Company. This private cartoon was penciled as a birthday card to a brother in 1949.

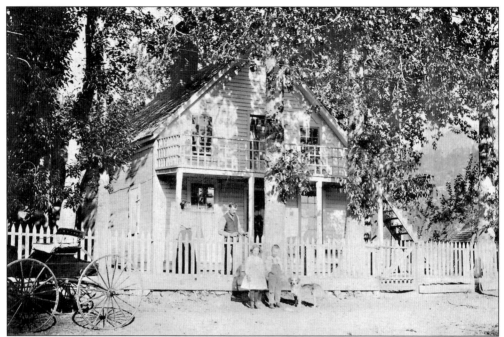

John and Mary Hawkins were Mormons and among the earliest settlers in Woodfords. Their grandson Harry Hawkins told of a meeting Mary once had with Brigham Young. The Mormon leader came to her one day saying a vision told him John would have to take more wives. She retorted: "Listen, Brigham, I had a vision, too, and John ain't gonna take any more wives!" This photograph is of Mary Hawkins's house, Diamond Ranch, probably taken in the late 19th century.

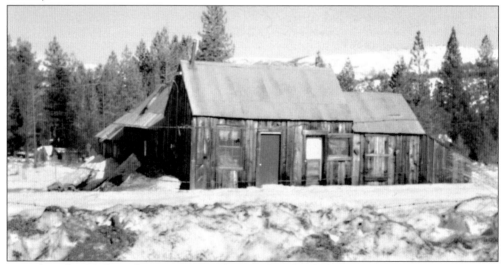

Regarding the Washo Indians, Harry Hawkins said: "I think they were some of the best people we had around us." Henry Rupert, a Washo shaman known as Moses, told Hawkins that Indians cannot become white men. They want to live in the wild and be free. Hawkins explained: "They don't want to be shackled up with the white people's ways. I don't blame them. I think we ought to back up ourselves a little on a lot of things." This photograph shows Harry Hawkins's house, which still stands at the head of Diamond Valley.

Four

THE MIDDLE YEARS
WHERE DID EVERYONE GO?

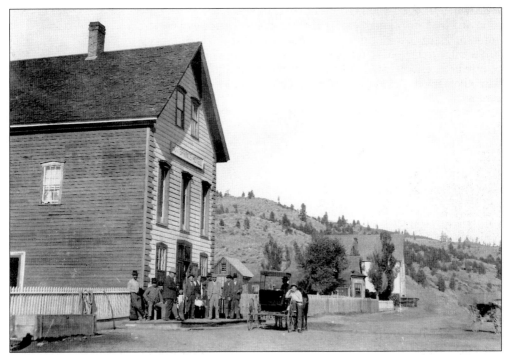

In 1883, Alvin Merrill Grover moved the Old Fiske House from Silver Mountain to Markleeville, thus establishing the Hot Springs Hotel. Several townspeople gathered for this photograph, taken in front of the hotel in its new location in Markleeville. The hotel attracted tourists who came to enjoy the high mountain air and restorative mineral waters in Hot Springs Valley. Later the name of the hotel was changed to the Alpine Hotel. The building is still standing and houses the Wolf Creek restaurant and Cutthroat Saloon on the corner of Highway 89 and Montgomery Street in Markleeville.

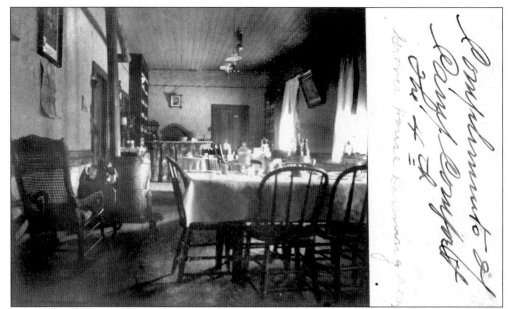

Pictured here is the Grover Hotel Dining Room as it looked in a 1904 postcard. It was a family-style establishment, frequented by miners, ranchers, townspeople, and visitors to Markleeville. It was known for its friendly atmosphere and wholesome food.

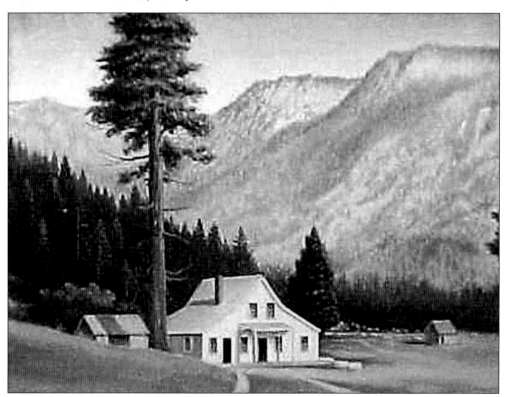

The Alvin Merrill Grover ranch in beautiful Hot Springs Valley was developed near the hot springs. Today the springs, named for the Grover family, are part of the California State Park System.

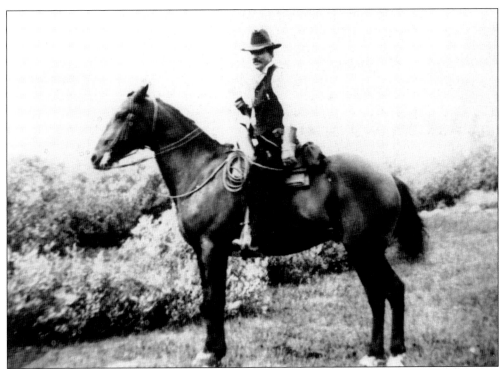

Charles A. Grover, Alvin Merrill Grover's son, was Alpine County sheriff from 1898 to 1913. Maintaining law and order was not always an easy job, especially when miners or rough-and-tumble ranch hands decided to liven things up.

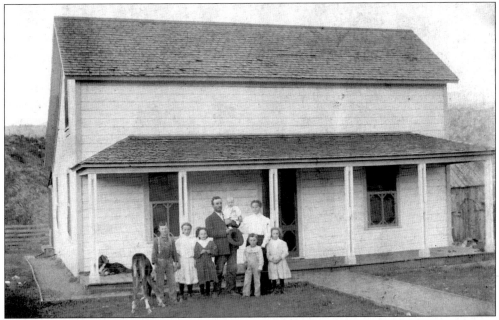

The Grover family is pictured in front of their home, built by Charles A. Grover in 1899. A note on the back of the photograph says, "Moved the structure from Silver Mountain, was the old schoolhouse. Papa paid $18.00 for lumber."

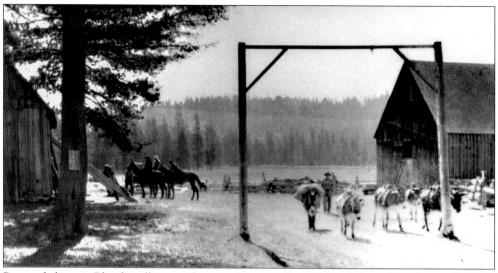

Pictured above is Blood's tollgate and station house in Bear Valley. The toll road, completed by Harvey Spaulding Blood and his partner in the mid-1860s between Silver Mountain and Big Trees in Calaveras County, was the silver mining area's main route to the western Sierra Gold Country. (Courtesy of Eric Jung)

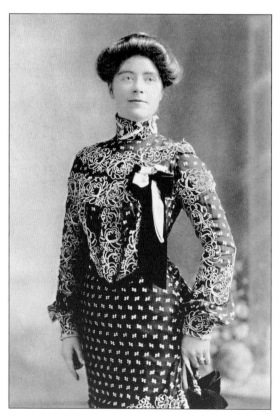

Reba Blood of Bear Valley, a poised young matron, was the daughter of Harvey Blood and his wife, Elizabeth. Reba moved away from her family to live in San Francisco when she married a banker in 1902. (Courtesy of the Calaveras Historical Society.)

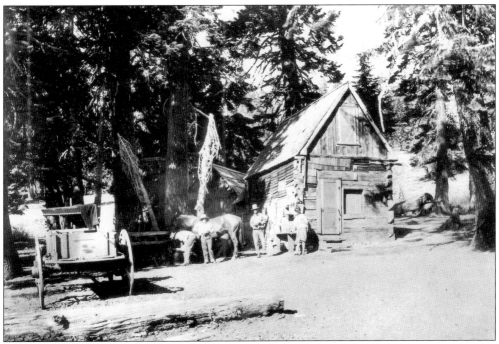

This rustic cabin was located in Tryon Meadows in the scenic Highland Lakes area west of Ebbetts Pass, near Bear Valley.

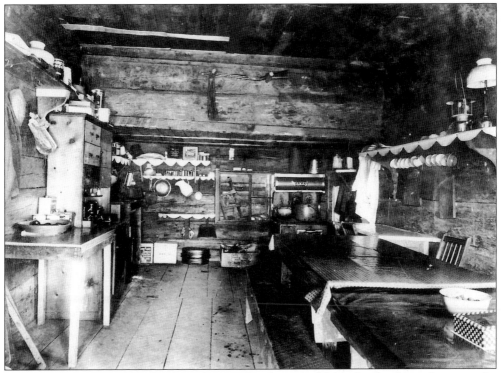

The interior of the Highland Lakes cabin typifies the rugged lifestyle of early residences in the Highland-Bear Valley area of Alpine County.

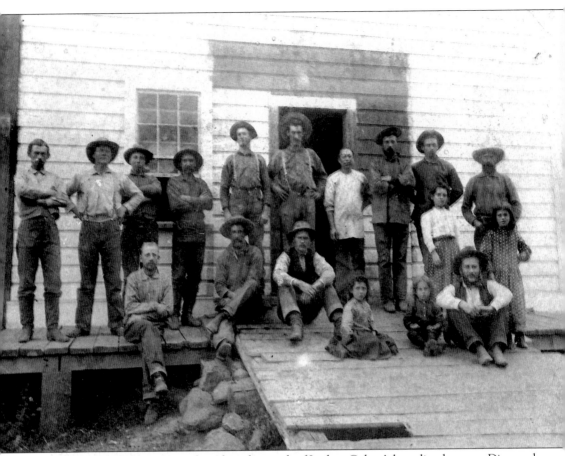

Lodgers and neighbors are gathered on the porch of Isadore Cohen's boarding house at Diamond Sawmill near Woodfords. Although the exact date of this photograph is not known, by the time it was taken around 1870, Woodfords had long been established as a transportation hub for busy stage and mail routes. Located at the junction of Carson Canyon and Markleeville Road (roughly the junction of present-day Highways 88 and 89) the accommodations at Woodfords served travelers going to and from Placerville, California and Genoa, Nevada.

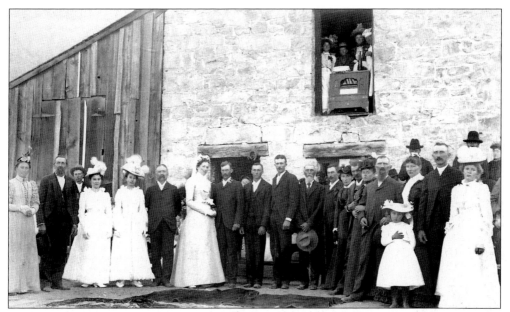

In the latter 19th century, June was apparently as popular for weddings as it is today. The wedding of Stella Bassman and William Stodieck took place on June 21, 1899, at the Bassman-Gansberg ranch in Fredericksburg. The birth name of the bride was Johanna Louise Adele, but she was affectionately called Della, not Stella, as reported by the *Courier* of Gardnerville, Nevada.

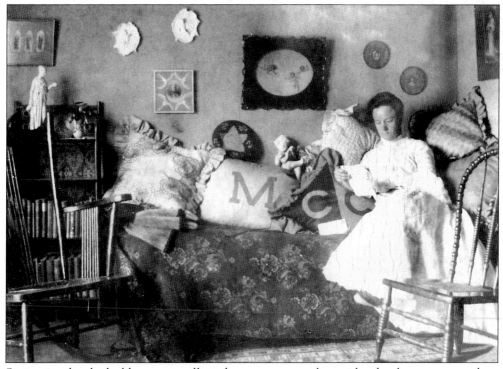

Sitting in what looks like a cozy college dorm room, complete with school mementos such as pennants and letters, Agnes Wiley reads a letter. Agnes came all the way from Los Angeles to teach school in Markleeville in about 1905.

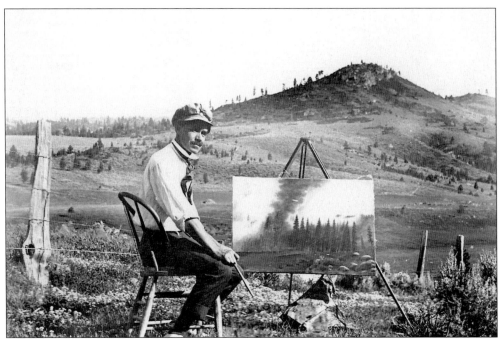

Walt Monroe was a local artist who painted many landscapes depicting Markleeville and the surrounding Sierra Nevada. The painting in this photograph is one of a fire in the Mono National Forest, which includes eastern Alpine County. Several Monroe paintings are on display in the Alpine County Museum.

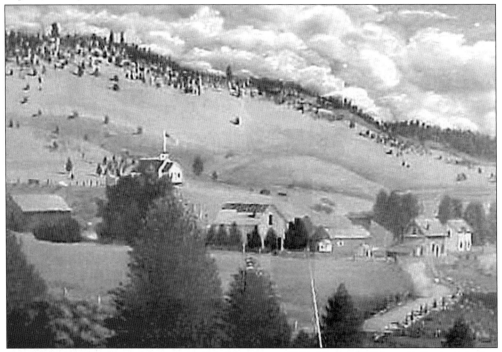

Seen above is Walt Monroe's painting of Markleeville, c. 1900. Note the Webster School on the low hill and the lack of pine trees above the school, due to clear cutting in the area 25 years earlier.

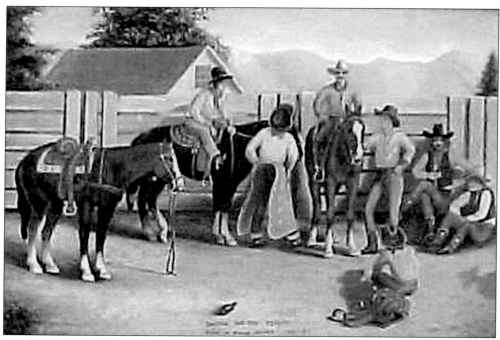

Local artist Walt Monroe depicts Alpine County cowboys in this *c*. 1900 painting.

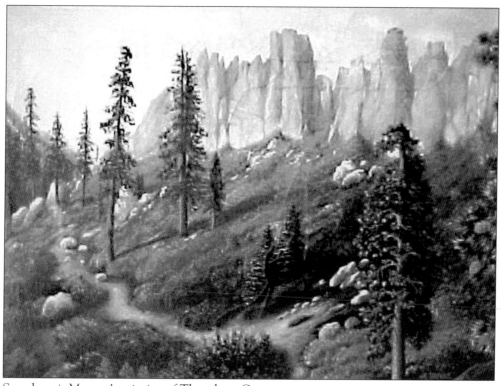

Seen here is Monroe's painting of Thornburg Canyon.

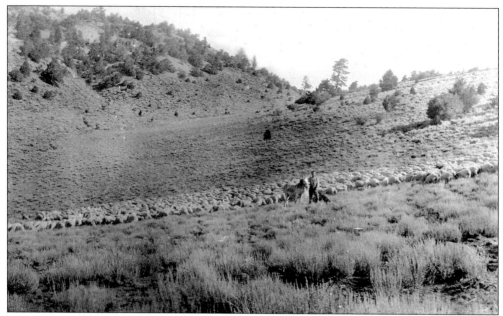

Cattle and sheep were herded into the high mountain meadows of the Sierra to graze during the summer months. This sheep herd is pictured grazing at Monitor Pass (8,314 feet in elevation) near Heenan Lake.

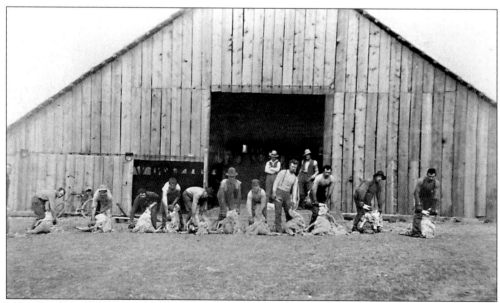

This photograph shows a sheep-shearing crew on Henry Neddenriep's ranch, now owned by the Gansberg family.

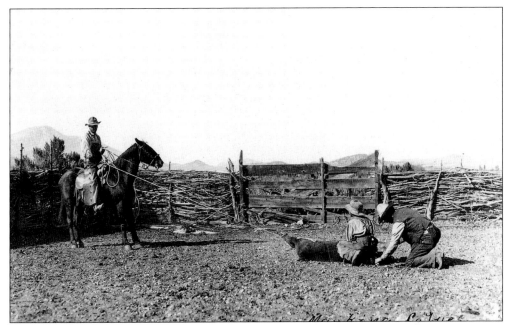

Ranching was an arduous livelihood for many families living in Alpine County. One of the jobs was branding or cutting an ear notch in animals new to the herds.

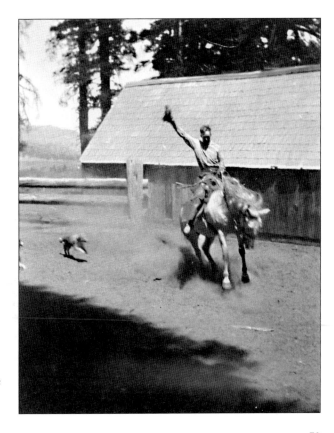

Ray Kenny is breaking one of the Dressler's broncos at the Dressler Cow Camp in Charity Valley.

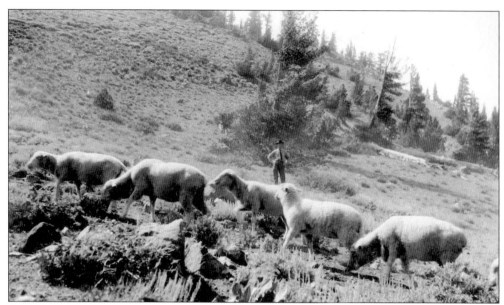

Keeping rancher's livestock healthy was a major job for the veterinarian. Dr. Dye is shown inoculating sheep for hoof-and-mouth disease near Heenan Lake.

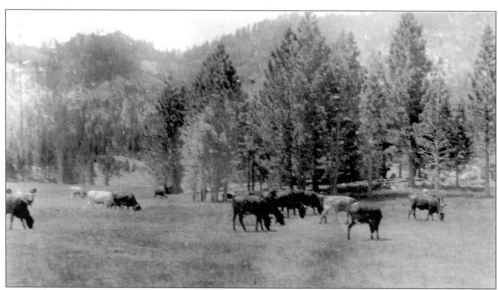

Silver Mountain, Alpine County's first boom-and-bust mining town and county seat, became this peaceful mountain scene following its decline in the latter 1870s. By the early 1920s, the Isabella boarding house in Silver Mountain was torn down. Its lumber was used to construct Scossa's Cow Camp, a rustic assemblage still visible along Highway 4, about a mile east of the Silver Mountain town site.

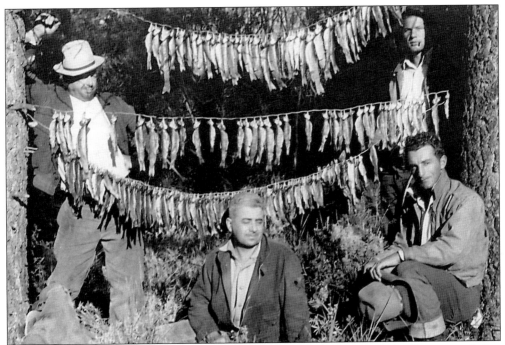

Looking at these trout stringers, one can see why Alpine County was—and still is—regarded as an excellent place to fish and hunt. These fishing buddies certainly caught their limit, if there was one!

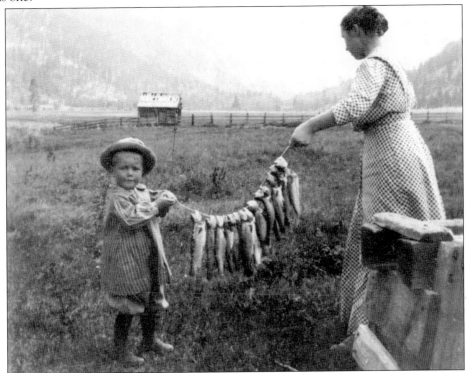

In the "good old days" a fishing creel was hardly big enough to hold your catch.

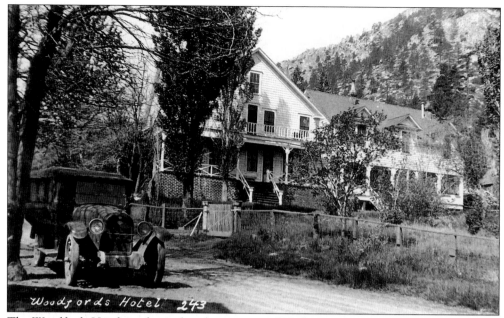

The Woodfords Hotel was located at the junction of Highways 88 and 89. This Model A Ford, a sign of the times, was parked in front of the hotel. The old hotel is gone, replaced by a bed-and-breakfast inn called "The Mountain and the Garden," owned by Alpine County native Linda Merrill.

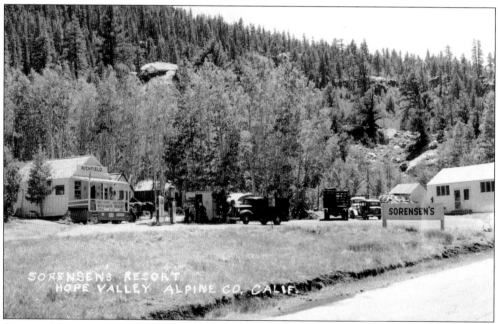

Sorenson's Resort, situated along Highway 88 in Hope Valley, was a popular vacation spot with cabins and amenities. It is still a popular destination both in winter and summer. The resort has gone through several transformations over the years and features quaint Scandinavian-style cabins and winding paths through the aspen trees surrounding the complex.

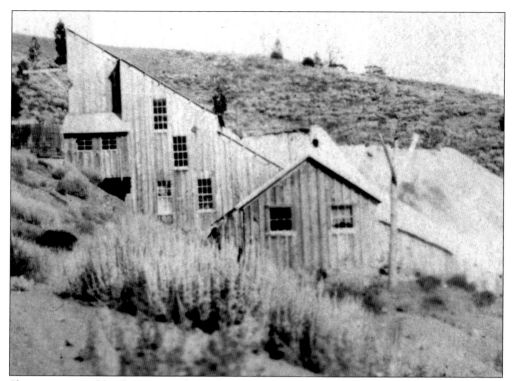

Shipping ore and lumber was costly, and noisy quartz and lumber mills once dotted the Alpine mining areas. The Alpine Mill rambled down the hillside towards the East Fork of the Carson River, just beyond Eagle Gulch.

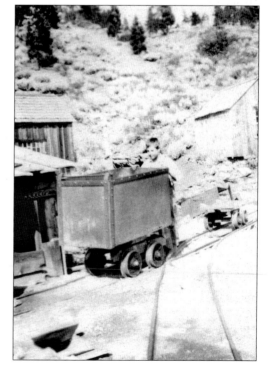

In its heyday, the Morning Star Mine was one of the major patents anchoring the Mogul Mining District. But, as with most of the ores found in Alpine County, processing it was difficult and expensive. The mine was purchased by Lewis "Lord" Chalmers in 1882, when the technology to process this type of ore became more advanced. Under Chalmers ownership, the Morning Star produced about 700 tons of ore, made some money, and then was abandoned.

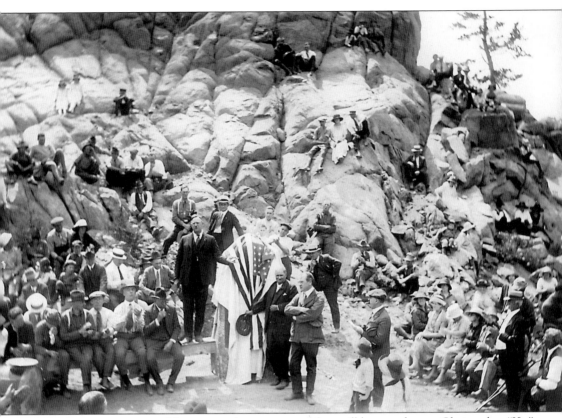

There are many sites and features in the area named for trailblazer and scout Christopher "Kit" Carson: Carson Pass, the Carson River, Nevada's Carson Valley and its capital, Carson City. During a mid-winter crossing of the Sierra by the John C. Fremont party in 1844, Carson jumped into an icy river near the high mountain pass to help Fremont, who had fallen in. Fremont later named the pass in Carson's honor. The Kit Carson monument, located at the crest of Carson Pass on Highway 88, was dedicated June 23, 1926. Its design features the pattern of a blaze cut into a nearby tree trunk by Carson. The original blaze was removed in 1888, and is on display at Sutter's Fort. The dedication ceremony, pictured here, was well attended, and included state and local dignitaries.

Five

TRANSITION

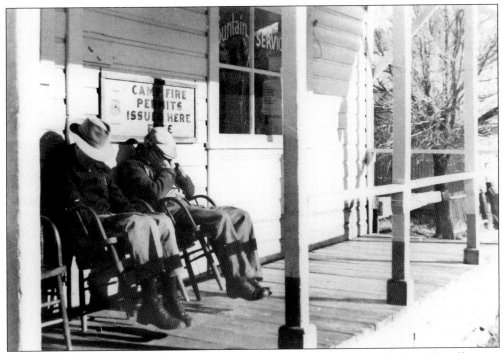

Members of the "Sit and Spit Club," c. 1945, live up to their name on the Markleeville store porch. When the mining and timber industries began to fail in Alpine County, the population declined. Ranchers, a few small businesses, and the Washo Indians remained, and life grew quiet. Grazing cattle and sheep took advantage of abundant mountain meadows. The elements, always dramatic in the high Sierra, starred in their own chapters of the county's history. But as the 20th century progressed, leisure activities became more prominent, and Alpine County gained renown for its recreational resources. Facilitating camping, hunting, fishing, hiking, and skiing became the economic base of the county.

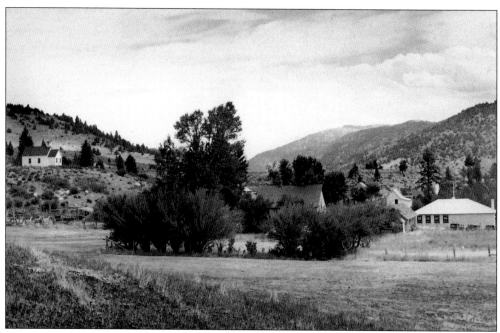

A broad landscape of Markleeville in the early 1930s features the old Webster School on the hill and the new Webster School on the right.

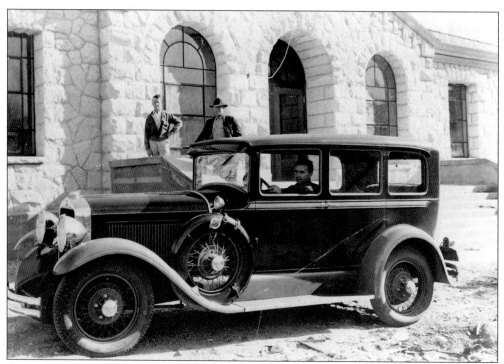

Alpine County supervisor Grant Merrill, who was also an engineer for the California Division of State Highways, is pictured standing to the left of Sheriff Charlie Barrett on the steps of the just-completed Alpine County Courthouse in 1928.

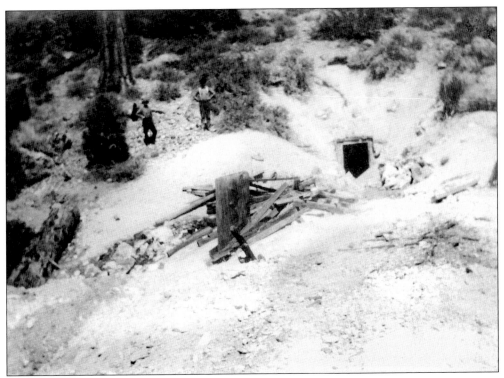

This is the portal of the original tunnel at the Leviathan Mine, atop the ridge on the north side of Monitor Pass. The Leviathan produced three minerals in its working life: silver, copper, and sulfur. Sulfur mining created ecological problems in the watershed that require treatment and monitoring to the present day.

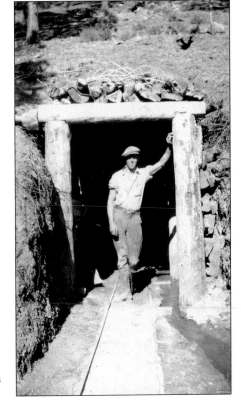

John Barrett stands at the mouth of the Leviathan Mine in its silver-producing era.

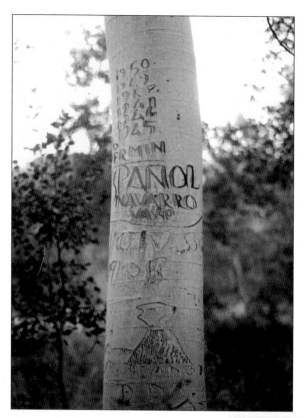

Basque artists, working as sheepherders, filled the aspen groves of Alpine County with arborglyphs representing themes in their lives. Crude printing or elegant script is carved into the soft bark of aspen trunks, memorializing the loneliness of the sheepherders' solitary existence, philosophies, anecdotes of friendship, and personal histories with names, dates, and hometowns of the artists. Illustrations depict women's faces and body parts, self portraits, birds, and animals, such as coyotes snatching lambs.

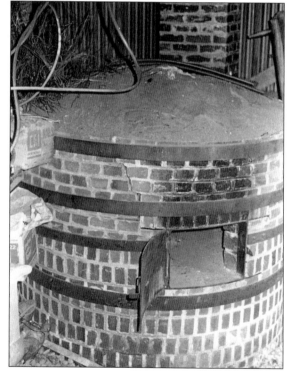

At right is a Basque oven in an abandoned cabin on Dangberg's sheep ranch at the head of Hope Valley. The wood-fired oven was used to bake bread, pies, meat, and stews for sheepherders in the valley. Stoked early in the morning, it was kept hot by banking fresh hot coals along the brick walls while the food baked in the center.

Basque carvings were done throughout the aspen groves of Alpine County. Even trees in the most remote stands were decorated. But why were messages placed on trees that most of the population would never see? The answer is that in many instances they were intended to be seen only by fellow herders. This explains why trees feature personal information including names, dates, ethnic identities, towns, and provinces, as well as drawings that may illustrate "shepherding news" or more intimate information. Since companies recruited herders from various valleys in the Western Pyrenees Mountains in Europe, the backgrounds and even language of herders differed from outfit to outfit and hence grove to grove. As time goes by there is less chance of deciphering the secrets of the trees, as bark growth distorts the images. Pictured here is a carving of a woman on a white fir tree in the Blue Lakes area of Hope Valley.

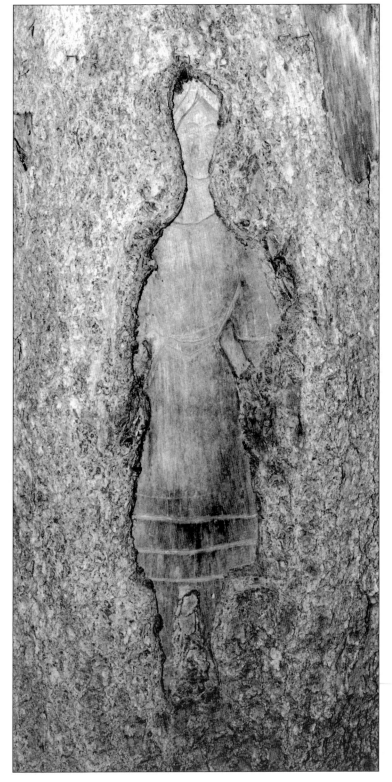

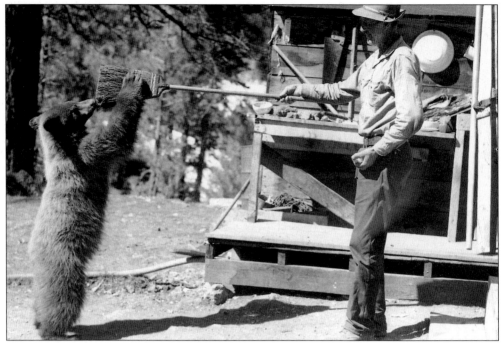

John Thornburg, caretaker of the Leviathan Mine in 1951, was photographed amusing himself and the photographer with what appears to be a docile black bear cub—at least until mama arrived on the scene!

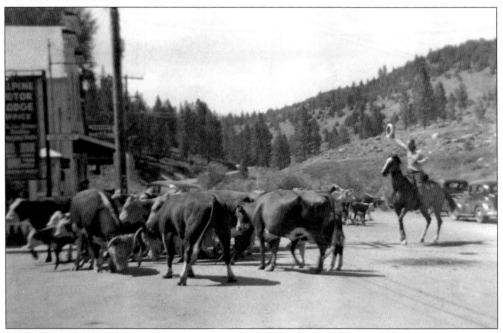

Some things never change: the Alpine Hotel is seen here in 1955 on the left at the corner of Main Street (Highway 89) and Montgomery Street. Fred Gansberg is shown herding cattle in downtown Markleeville. This wasn't an easy job, especially if the cattle didn't want to cooperate. The two bulls in front are about to lock horns.

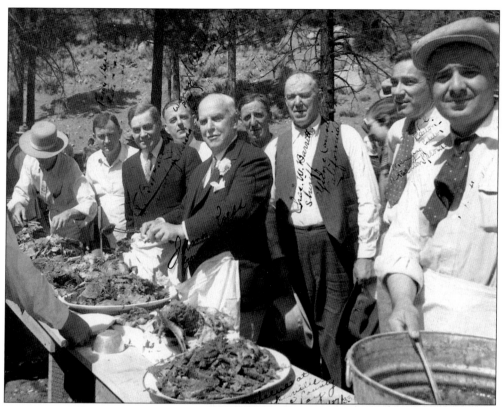

Sheriff Charlie Barrett hosted a barbeque spread for the governors of California and Nevada, James Rolph and F. B. Balzar, respectively. Governor Rolph, looking ready to "tuck it in," is standing in front of Sheriff Barrett.

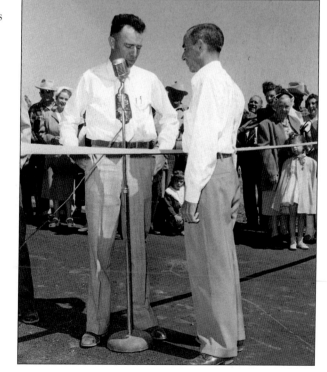

Several dignitaries attended this 1954 dedication of Monitor Pass (Highway 89). County supervisor Hubert Bruns is facing the camera. (Courtesy of the California Department of Transportation.)

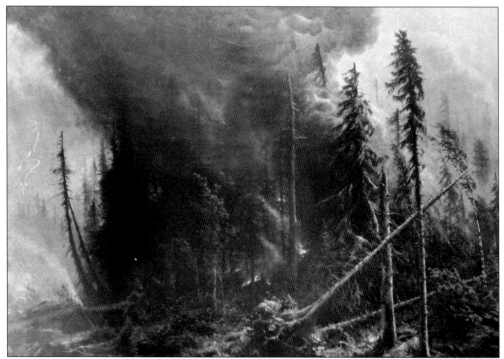

Wildfire is a constant threat during the Sierra dry seasons. This Walt Monroe painting depicts a blaze in old-growth forest in Alpine County.

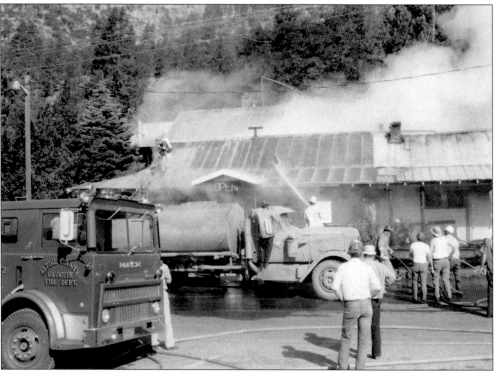

Members of the Alpine County Volunteer Fire Department fight a structural blaze in July 1979.

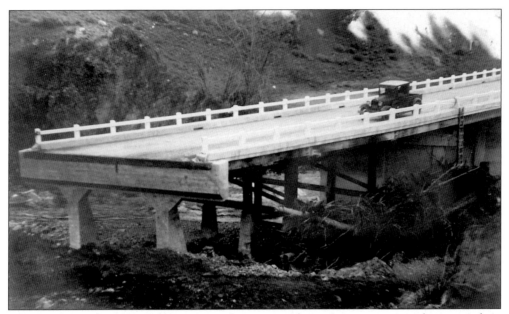

Regularly beleaguered by floods since its formation, Alpine County copes with nature's fury. Pictured above is the washed-out approach to Hangman's Bridge, south of Markleeville.

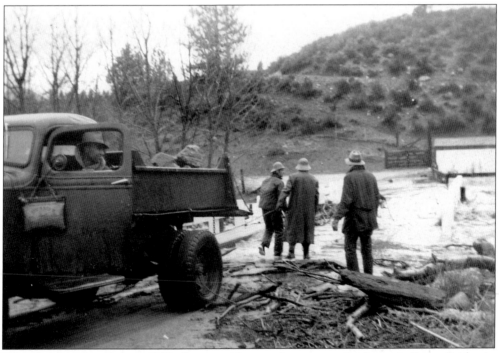

This photograph, taken in 1950, shows residents trying to save the Laramie Street Bridge in Markleeville from rising floodwater.

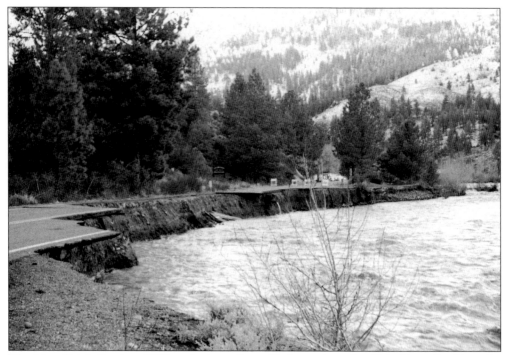

The New Year's flood in 1997 washed out State Highway 4 south of Markleeville. Here the view upstream on the East Fork of the Carson River shows why Highway 89 and Highway 4 were not drivable.

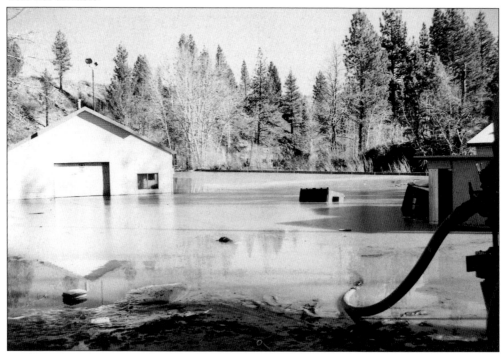

In 1997, Markleeville Creek overflowed onto the U.S. Forest Service compound in Markleeville. This photograph shows water being pumped from the area.

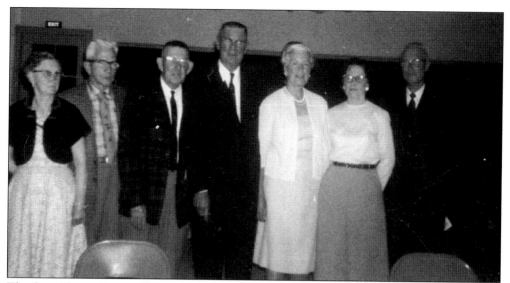

The first Alpine County Historical Society Board of Directors met on June 19, 1963, to chart the course of preserving Alpine County's rich heritage. From left to right are Lillian Thornburg (secretary), L. A. Love (director), Al Chain (vice-president and director), L. C. Wiese (president), Ada Currie (treasurer), Zella Mann (director), and Philip Brooks (installing officer).

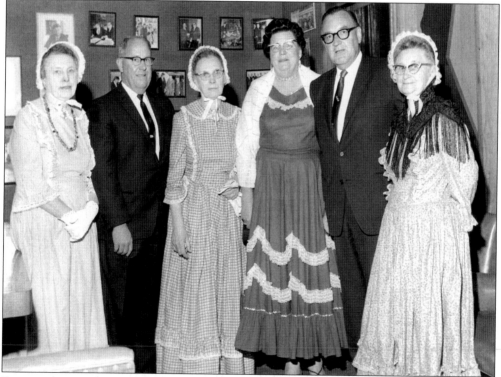

Representatives of the Alpine County Historical Society in period costume meet with Gov. Pat Brown and Sen. William Symons Jr. in Sacramento in 1964. The occasion honored Alpine County's centennial celebration. From left to right are Lillian Egger, Sen. Symons, Sophie Peters, Lucile Chain, Governor Brown, and Lillian Thornburg.

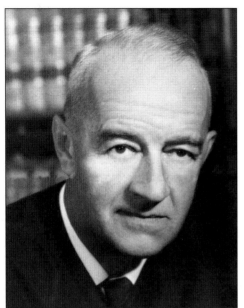

Judge George Francis earned money to attend UC Berkeley and Boalt Law School by toting a shotgun and a .45 as a guard for Wells Fargo express trains. Appointed superior court judge in Alpine County in 1948, he heard only three jury cases during his 13-year term, all others being settled before coming to court. Called a genius at settlements by California's chief justice, Francis was still sitting as a trial judge after 40 years at age 87.

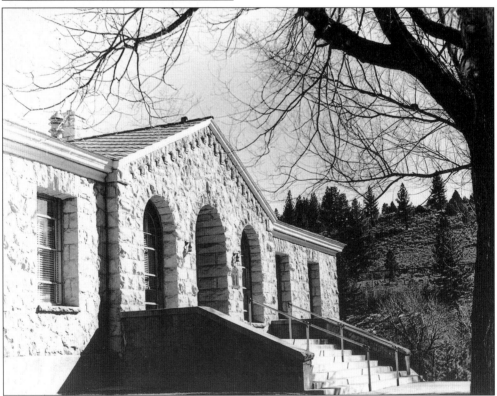

Judge Francis recalled that county residents believed in personal responsibility. In each personal injury case he heard, the juries found for the defendant. In one case the plaintiff fell off a pack horse and was suing the packer. A jurist for this trial, upon being asked if there was any reason he could not be fair and impartial, replied, "No, except I find in this situation the horse is usually right."

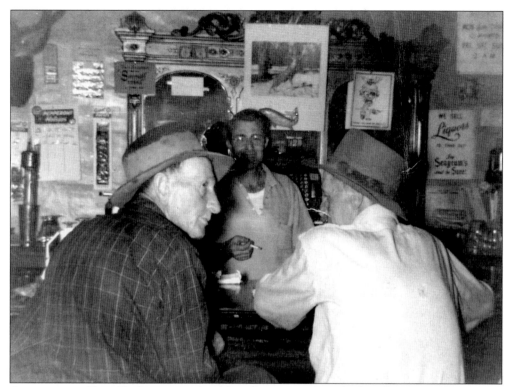

Congressman Claire Engle, running hard for office, stepped inside the Alpine Hotel bar. Seeing only one man, he grandly told the bartender, "Let's everybody have a drink." The bartender stepped away and Engle thought he heard something like a dinner triangle. As he described the ensuing scene, "All these people came out of the brush and there were twenty fellows in there." In 1954, Howard Dickson, Doug Ford, and Walt Thornburg wait for the congressman to return to the Alpine Hotel bar.

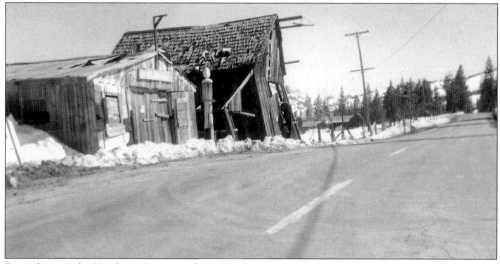

Seen above is the Hawkins Garage and Gas Station prior to its demolition in 1969. This photograph, taken from the middle of Highway 89, illustrates that the hamlet's businesses had fallen into disrepair in this era.

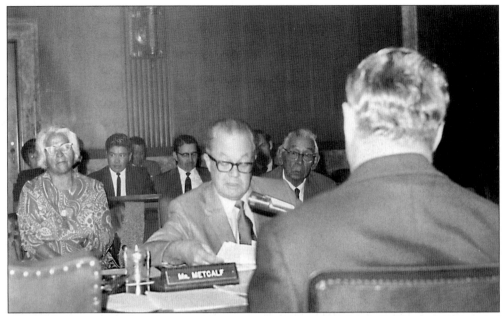

In 1970, 120 years after Euro-Americans began appropriating their land, the Hung a lel ti band of the Washo Indians was allotted 80 acres for a community in Woodfords. The process of acquiring the land took eight years. This photograph, taken during Senate hearings in Washington, D.C., shows two Woodfords residents who were instrumental in the procurement, tribal secretary Belma Jones on the left, and tribal chair Earl James on the right of Sen. Lee W. Metcalf of Montana.

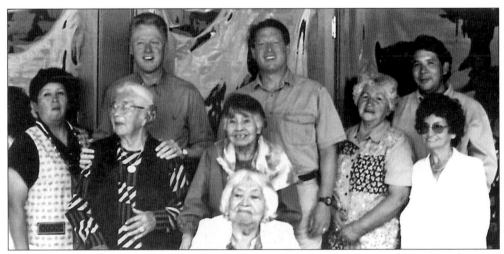

In August 1997, members of the Washo Language Circle attended a meeting at Lake Tahoe and spoke with Pres. Bill Clinton and Vice Pres. Al Gore. At that time, the tribe was given 400 acres of land, encompassing the meadows behind Meeks Bay, where traditional medicinal plants once flourished. Woodfords residents in the contingent included Amy Barber in the front and Eloise James on the left.

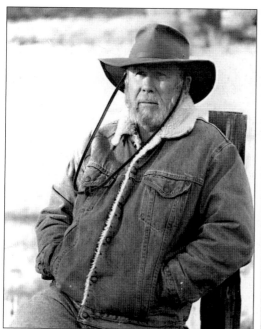
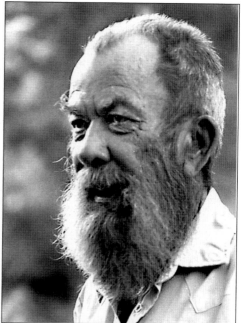
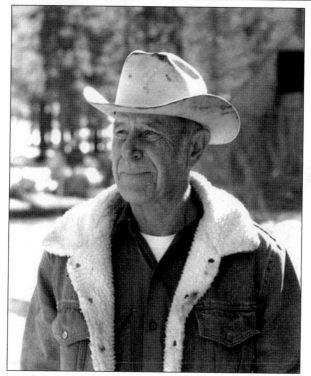

These sons of pioneer stock came when the silver mines were only a memory and the automobile had replaced the horse. Gary Coyan (above left), Jim Lyons (above right), and Fritz Thornburg (bottom) were raised to fish Markleeville Creek and hunt in the mountains of Alpine County.

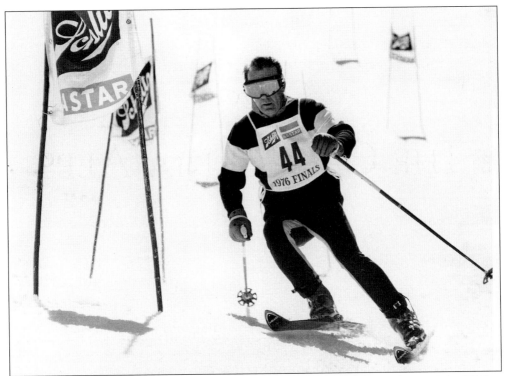

Because he competed in downhill skiing competitions, Stuart Merrill was nicknamed the "Skiing Sheriff of the Sierra." After serving five terms as sheriff, from 1958 to 1978, he retired to serve on the Alpine County Board of Supervisors.

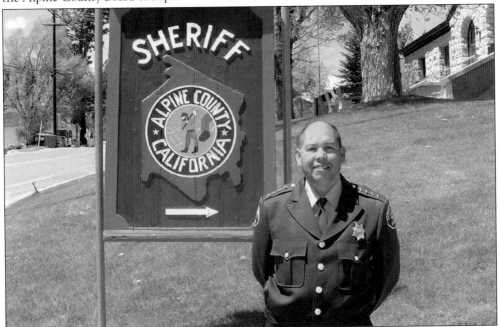

John Crawford was elected sheriff of Alpine County in 2002. A Washo, he is the first Native American to become sheriff of a county in California history.

Six

THE CALIFORNIA ALPS

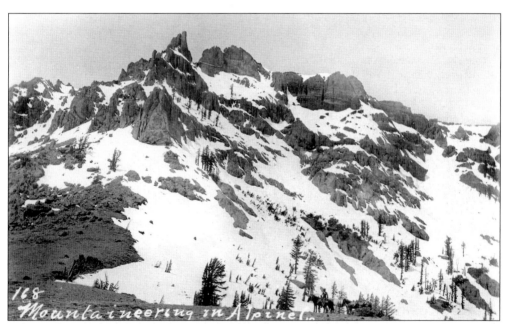

168
Mountaineering in Alpine.

Above timberline, the peaks of Alpine County's massive mountains are polished and scored by glaciation and weather. Scandinavians named this 775-square-mile section of the eastern Sierra Nevada Range, "Alpine," because it reminded them of the Alps. It is half boreal region—comprised of lodge pole pine, red fir, aspen, and mountain hemlock—and half Jeffery pine region. It has more than 60 high-mountain lakes, ranging in size from substantial, navigable bodies of water to small, pure glacial pools. Over 20 peaks rise above 9,000 feet. Recreational activities in what is commonly referred to as the "California Alps" include hiking, camping, nature study, fishing, hunting, canoeing, river rafting, cycling, mountain biking, snow mobile riding, and downhill and cross-country skiing.

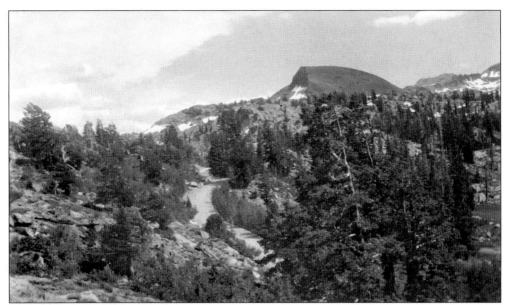

The mountains of the Sierra Nevada Range increase in altitude from 2,000 to 3,000 feet in the north. To the south, Mt. Whitney and 12 others rise to more than 14,000 feet. The mountain passes throughout the range also increase in altitude from north to south. In Alpine County, the northernmost is Luther Pass at 7,740 feet. Carson Pass, shown here, is 8,573 feet, and southernmost is Ebbetts Pass at 8,730 feet.

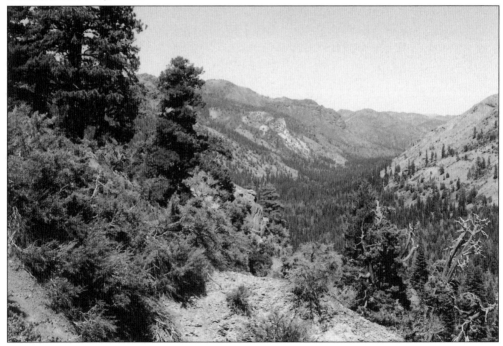

On the western side of the 360-mile-long Sierra Nevada Range, hills rise in a two to six percent gradation; but the crest is near the eastern border. From it rock walls fall precipitously, ending in valleys 4,000 feet in elevation. Eastern Alpine County is a wilderness of sculpted peaks, canyons, meadows, and lakes.

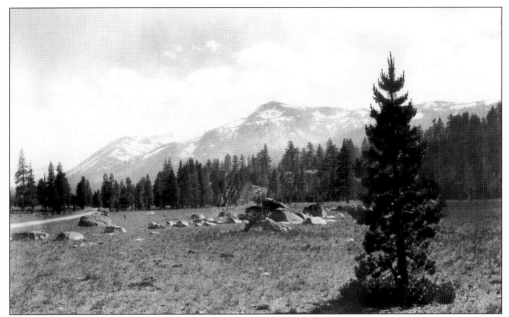

Carson Pass was named for Kit Carson, who traversed it with mountain man Thomas Fitzpatrick while leading the Fremont expedition to Alta California in the winter of 1844. Approaching the pass on February 4th, they struggled through deep snow. Fremont reported, "The summit line presented a range of naked peaks, apparently destitute of snow and vegetation; but below, the face of the whole country was covered with timber of extraordinary size."

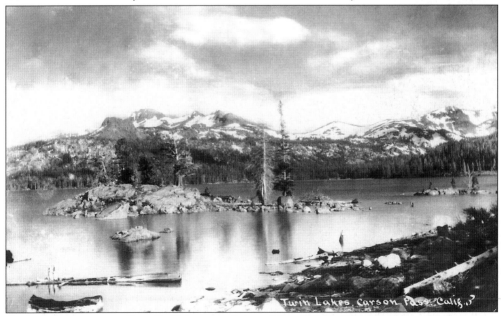

Caples Lake was originally called Mountain Lake or Nevada Lake. It was later named Twin Lakes because in dry years, there were two bodies of water with a strip of land between. Once dammed, with the separating land submerged, the lake was named Caples after Dr. James Caples, whose block house, with logs locked at the corners, became a stopping place for travelers. In 1879, "Doc" Caples represented the mountain district at California's second constitutional convention.

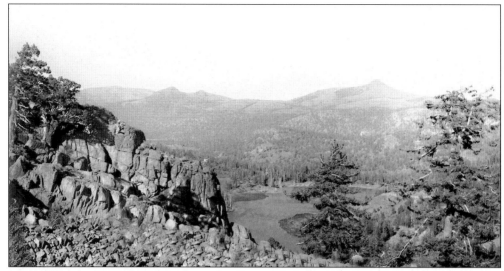

Mormons returning from California to the Great Salt Lake in 1848 took a whole day to move wagons and cattle from the summit of Carson Pass down the treacherous 800-foot Devil's Ladder. After the descent, they camped in a grassy, 7,000-foot-high valley and, having renewed hope for the success of their journey, named it Hope Valley.

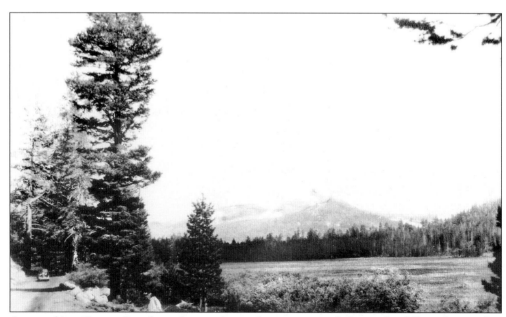

Approaching Carson Pass from the northeast, forty-niners and those who followed arrived at Hope Valley. They used it as a way-station to rest and gather strength before the last great push up the summit over Carson Pass and down into California.

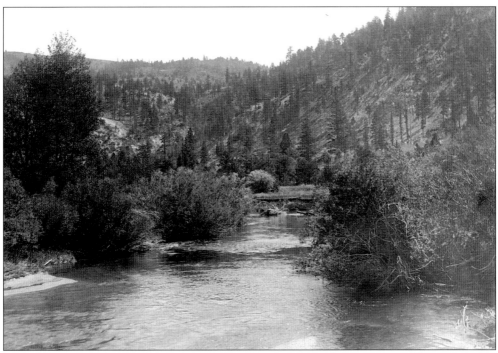

Alpine rivers and streams have served many purposes. Besides being fisheries, they are used as sources for canals that irrigate the fields of Alpine County and Carson Valley. Once they were the source of flumes that carried lengths of timber down steep mountainsides. They powered the stamp mills of Silver Mountain and the sawmills and grist mills of the East Carson River and Woodfords. In the glory days of mining, they transported thousands of cords of wood yearly to mines downstream. Sun-filled days following winter snow, ensures county streams remain full, providing holes for swimming, banks for picnicking, currents for kayaking, and havens for fishermen.

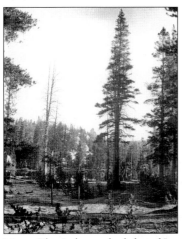 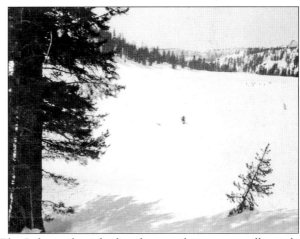

Upper Blue Lake on the left and Lower Blue Lake on the right, less than a mile apart, are collectively known as Blue Lakes. Curiously, the waters of Blue Lakes flow southward, being the source of the Mokelumne River, while nearby Lost Lake's water runs north to feed the East Carson River. In the late 1800s, Blue Lakes was a crossroads for various mining camps. Harmonial City was a prominent camp, located between the two lakes.

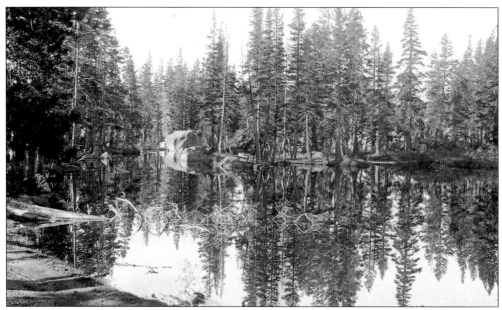

Border Ruffian Lake and Border Ruffian Road, now Blue Lakes Road off Highway 88, hosted a band of horse thieves operating in Alpine in the 1850s. The bandits stole horses from pioneers camped in Hope Valley, fattened the animals in secret meadows, and sold them to other immigrants making the trek. Border Ruffian Flats, off Blue Lakes Road, is also said to have been a hideout for the infamous Joaquin Murrieta gang.

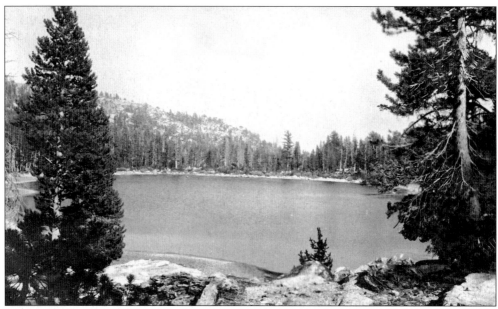

Burnside Lake is 5.5 miles east-northeast of Carson Pass, along Hot Springs Creek. According to local legend, it was named for Gen. Ambrose E. Burnside, the famous Union general in the Civil War. This is likely, since during the war a company of Union troops was stationed in Markleeville to keep the county's silver out of Confederate coffers. Kayaking, canoeing, and fishing for brook and rainbow trout have long been recreational activities in the lake.

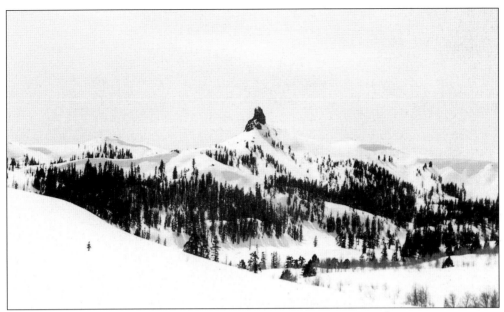

This scene shows winter snows on 9,065-foot Jeff Davis Peak. Sierra Nevada means snowy range, and snow is an important climatic feature of Alpine County.

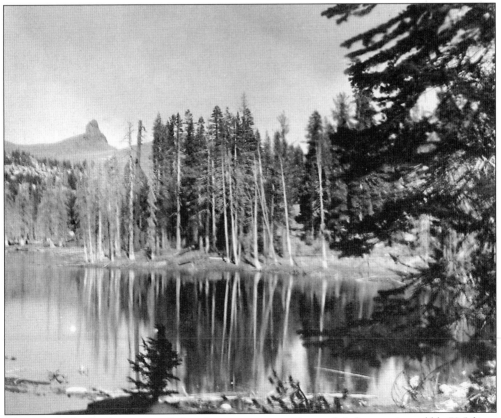

The greatest depth of snow recorded in the county was at Tamarack Lake—an incredible 73.5 feet.

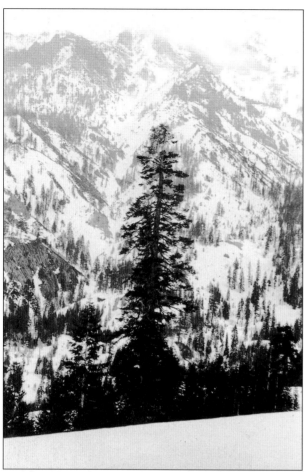

The first heavy winter recorded in Alpine County was in 1866–67. At Silver Mountain, avalanches caused buildings to be "crushed and knocked endways." In Hope Valley, 30 to 40 trees and immense boulders were swept from the mountains, and mail service and travel throughout the county were disrupted for weeks, as all roads in every direction were blocked. Below, Markleeville is shown in the winter of 1949, when snow covered the entire community.

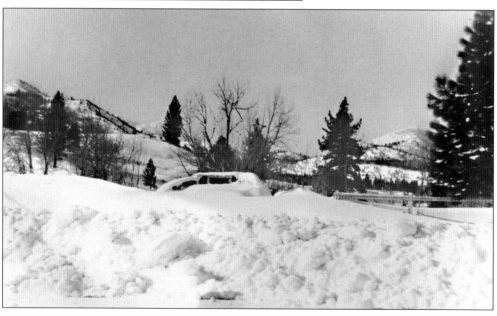

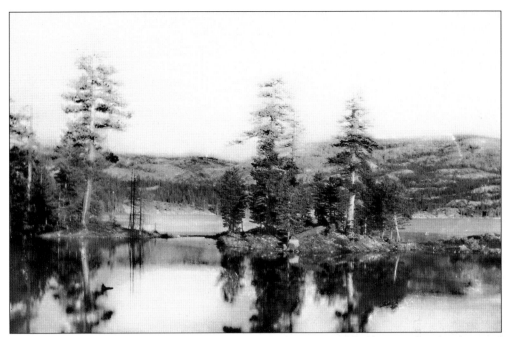

Many of the meadows of Alpine County are ancient lake basins filled by gravel and soil carried in streams that flow in. As time passed, plants of increasing size colonized the area, encroaching into the meadow and transforming it to forest.

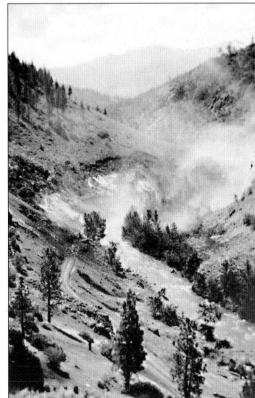

Alpine County's steep terrain, formidable winters, earthquake faults, periodic floods, and potential for wildfires make its landscape susceptible to change. Here a landslide on the East Fork of the Carson River below Monitor Pass is caught in a photograph in 1957. Massive flooding in 1955 precipitated the slide.

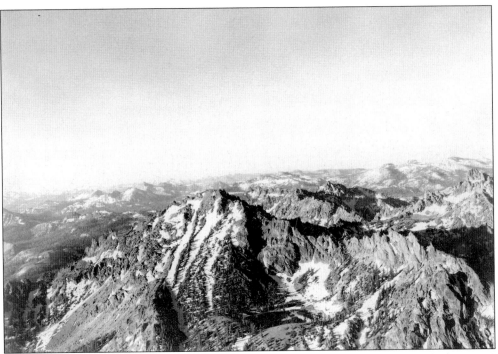

Saw-tooth, volcanic Raymond Peak rises 10,014 feet in the air. Pristine Raymond Lake lays 1,000 feet below.

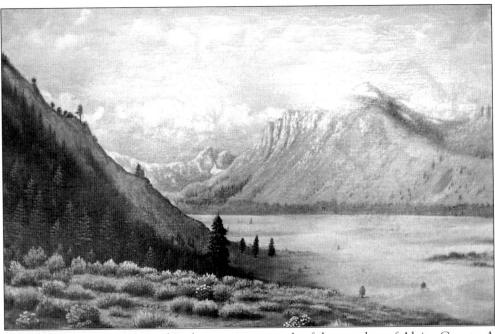

Pleasant Valley, below Raymond Peak, is a prime example of the grandeur of Alpine County. A creek with sandy beaches and pools for swimming or catch-and-release fishing runs through it. The terrain is perfect for cross-country ski treks in the winter or hiking when the snow melts. (Painting by Walt Monroe.)

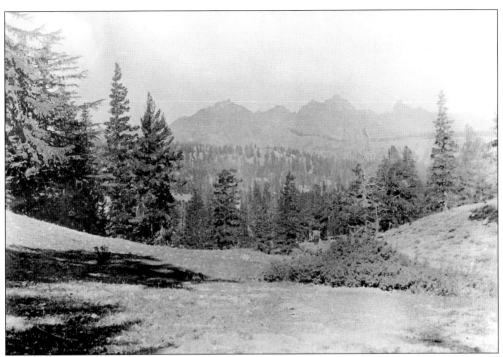

In 1916, having passed through the Calaveras Big Trees and crossed the 8,050-foot Pacific Grade Summit, new Highway 4 reached its eastern summit, Ebbetts Pass. In the distance, Reynolds Peak and its sisters filled the horizon. Ebbetts Pass was named in 1853 for John A. Ebbetts, who identified it as a potential route for a railroad across the Sierra Nevada Range. Ebbetts died in a steamboat boiler explosion near San Francisco in 1854, and the project was never undertaken.

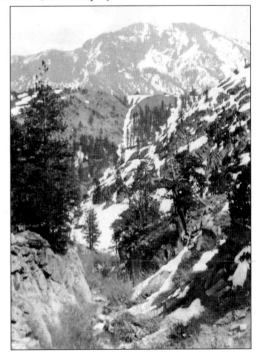

Massive Silver Mountain, rising to an altitude of 10,772 feet, is among the most prominent features of the California Alps. It features high meadows, craggy ridges, pines, streams, and brush above, and silver, galena, rutile, and andradite below ground. At its base, Silver Mountain, originally called Konigsberg, hosted Scandinavian miners as early as 1858.

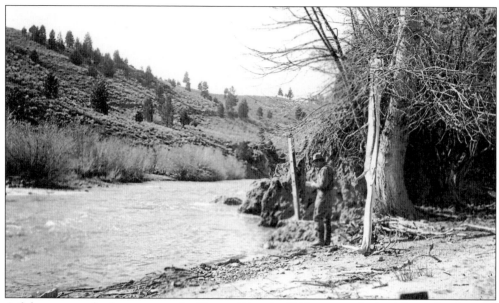

A fisherman angles for trout on the Carson River in 1916 against the backdrop of a clear-cut hillside. In 1876, renowned Comstock newsman Dan DeQuille, noting that pine-forested mountains previously allowed a gradual snow melt and year-round water flow, stated, "Already one bad effect of the denudation is seen in the summer failure of the water in the Carson river. The first spell of hot weather in the spring now sweeps nearly all the snow from the mountains and sends it down into the valleys in one grand flood."

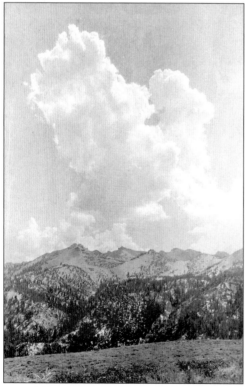

Below gathering thunderheads southeast of Monitor Pass, rises 10,800-foot Whitecliff Peak, and beneath it, dramatic Whitecliff Lake. In the distance is 10,022-foot Disaster Peak, named in 1877, when topographer W. A. Cowles accidentally dislodged a boulder on the peak and was severely injured.

Seven

ECHOES OF THE PAST

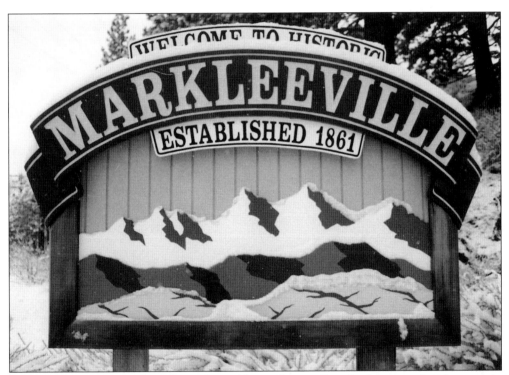

These are notable facts about Facts about Alpine County. It is the least populated county in California. It traditionally has the highest voter turnout in the state. Government agencies own 90 percent of the land, and only 10 percent is in private hands. Alpine County's Ed Schalbert was the last individual to hold the title of constable in California. Lucille Brown was one of the first females to hold the office of sheriff. Alpine is one of two counties in California without a railroad running through it. It has no incorporated cities. There are no stoplights in the county and no hospital or pharmacy.

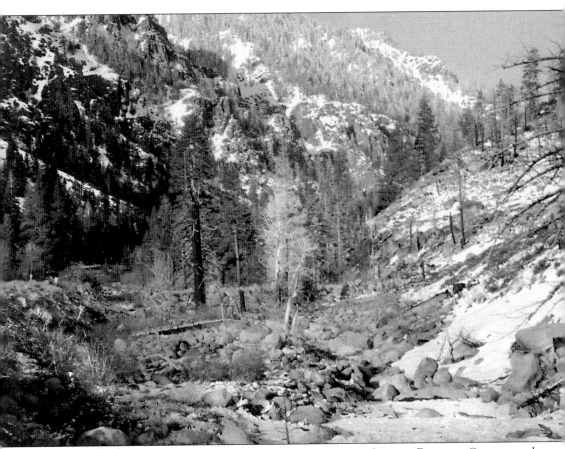

Woodfords Canyon was previously called Big Canyon, Carson Canyon, Emigrant Canyon, and Rocky Canyon. Its steep, narrow walls towered overhead, causing one female traveler to comment, "[It] seemed in some places almost to meet above our heads." The canyon was notoriously difficult to traverse, with large boulders, piles of fallen granite reportedly up to 300 feet high, and the Carson River, which had to be forded several times. Another immigrant said: "We were compelled to force our wagons over, around, and through many of those places by manual labor, the turns being too short to be made with the team hitched on." Still another told of breaking an axle, cutting the bed of the wagon to make a cart, and proceeding. In 1853, Lucky Bill Thorington joined with the man who founded Nevada's first settlement at Genoa, John Reese, to build a toll road through the canyon.

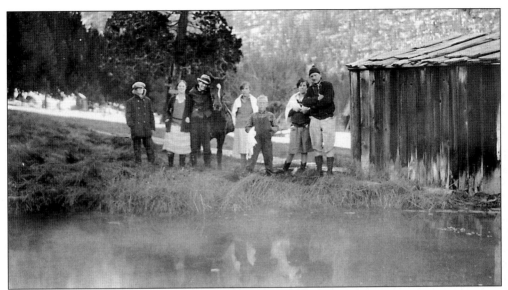

Grover Hot Springs is shown with the old bathhouse sometime before 1925. The springs are located 3.25 miles west of Markleeville, and have been a state park since 1959. The eight different springs that bubble from the earth at 140 degrees are channeled into a soaking pool at approximately 105 degrees. A swimming pool, kept considerably cooler, adjoins the hot spring. The spectacular meadow and mountains that surround the pools enhance the water's alleged therapeutic effects.

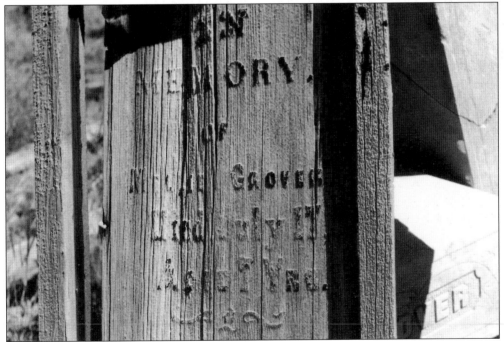

A wooden grave marker in the Markleeville Cemetery marks the resting place of Nellie Grover, aged 7 years. A. M. and Mary Grover's young daughter, one of three children, died of diphtheria on July 17, 1877. Besides ownership of their Markleeville Hotel and running the hot springs spa, the Grover's maintained a dairy in the hot springs meadow that supplied milk to area residents. They also held a patent to 5,000 acres of grazing land at Wolf Creek.

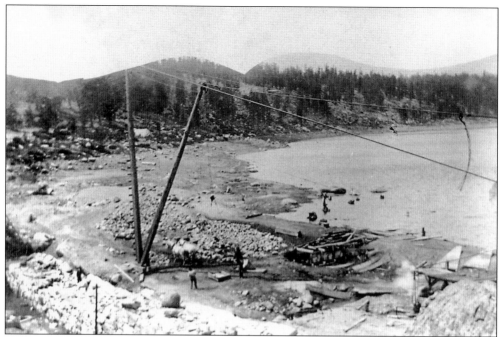

In the early 1920s, the dam at Caples Lake was built. It raised the water level more than 40 feet. Ironically, the home site of old Doc Caples, for whom the lake is named, was submerged when the water level rose.

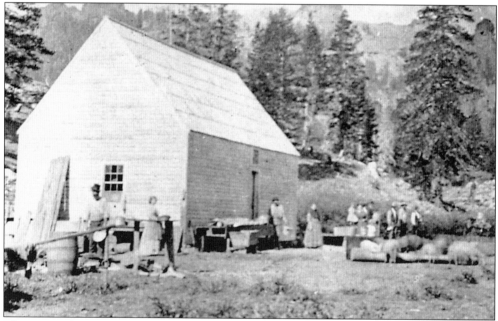

This picture shows the Kirkwood dairy, taken in the 1860s. Numerous meadows in Alpine County served as summer dairy lands. In 1860, the price of butter in Virginia City was $1 a pound. In 1867, it fell to 50 cents a pound, still a considerable sum if your cows were producing hundreds of pounds a week. In the background is 9,805-foot Thimble Peak, now the landmark for Kirkwood ski area's most challenging run.

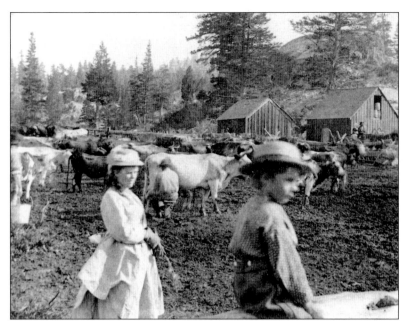

On June 15, 1867, the Alpine *Chronicle* reported, "On Monday last J. P. Scott and family, together with one hundred head of cattle arrived at his home in Hope Valley." The summer before, Scott's cows produced 400 to 500 pounds of butter a week which was sold in Virginia City and Gold Hill at 50 cents a pound. The young woman pictured in Scott's upper dairy might be Alice Scott, and the boy is possibly Edward Scott. If so, this was taken *c.* 1873.

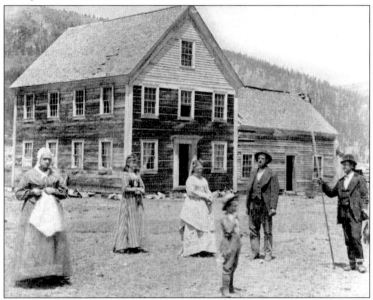

The Scotts' Hope Valley residence is shown about 1876. The individuals remain unidentified, but the 1870 census lists John P. Scott, 29; Alice Scott, 20; Edward Scott, 1; and Amos D. Scott, 26. Despite a productive mine, the "Old Billy Rogers," Hope Valley's real wealth came from its vast grasslands. Combined with the decline of the Comstock Lode and the improvement of Carson Valley's cattle ranges, the demand for dairy products diminished. And by 1880, the Scotts had moved on to greener pastures.

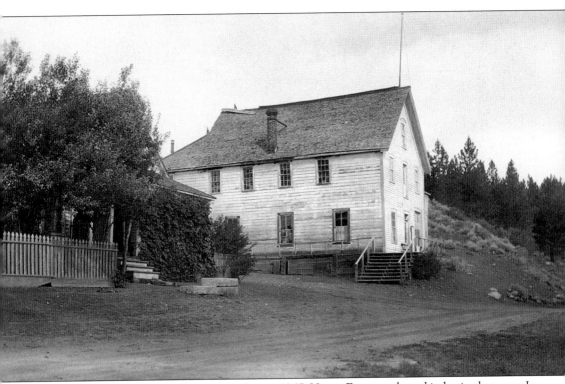

The Alpine County Court has operated since 1865. Henry Eno was elected judge in that year. In June 1869, he heard a case wherein a citizen had been arrested for stealing a gold watch and chain. When incarcerated, the prisoner tore off his clothes, broke up furniture, and attempted to burn down the jail. The accused was penitent in court, and Judge Eno, after advising him regarding future conduct, announced that the sentence would be lenient: three years at hard labor. The man flew into a rage, cussing and damning the judge. Judge Eno responded by adding four years to the sentence. The prisoner was taken away shouting: "G-d d—n you: you had better be dead when I come out again." Judge Eno ensured the threat would come to nothing. By the end of the year, struck by wanderlust, Eno moved on to prospect in various scattered mining districts. Shown here is the Odd Fellows building in Markleeville, the bottom floor of which was leased to the court after the county seat was moved here from Silver Mountain in 1875.

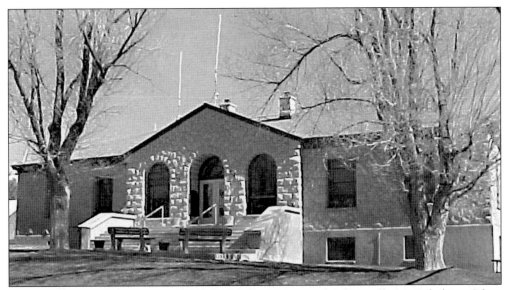

The Alpine County Courthouse was built in 1928, using rhyolite tuff quarried above Silver Mountain City. The architect was Frederic J. DeLongchamps, who built 500 buildings in or about Nevada, including seven courthouses. Under the courthouse cornerstone is a copper box with several items, including a telegram from Washington, D.C., two gold bonds, and a copy of an 1866 *Monitor Gazette*. The courthouse is a State Point of Historic Interest and is listed on the National Register of Historic Places.

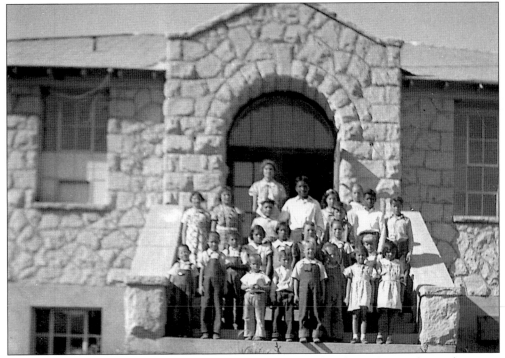

Enough stones were quarried to build a two-story courthouse, but due to financial considerations, the second story was not built. Instead, the stones were used to build the new Webster schoolhouse which is now the county library.

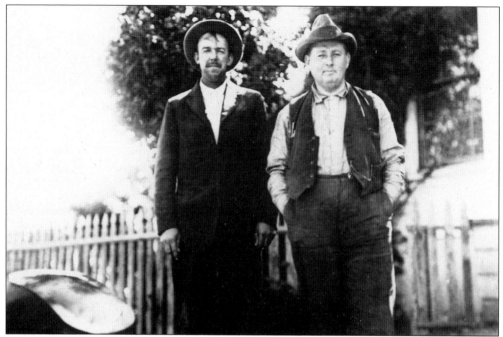

This 1920s photograph shows Sheriff Charles Barrett, who served 26 years, and county judge Lester Price. Rules of a county court are usually a phonebook-size document. Judge Price's Alpine County rules consisted of a pamphlet that could be inserted into a vest pocket.

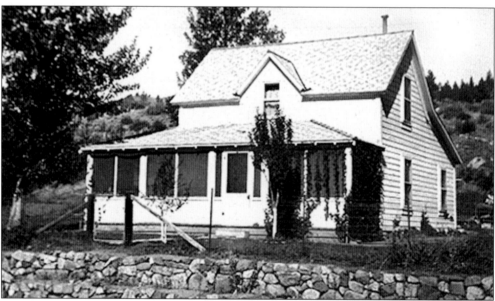

This is the last historic Markleeville home that has not been modified or destroyed, Local artist Walt Monroe and his father built it in 1907 as a wedding present for Walt's sister Lillian. Judge Lester T. Price bought the house in 1915, and the Price family still owns it. Judge Price allegedly had two rules in his court: first, all proceedings stopped at 4 o'clock, "no matter what;" and second, the court would take a vacation whenever necessary. The rules accommodated the judge's hobby—fly-fishing.

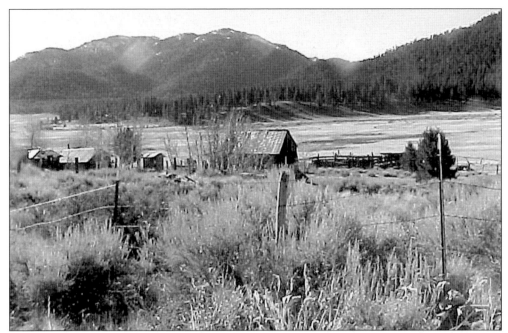

Vaquero Camp is located in Silver King Valley. Originally, the valley had a hotel that housed workers cutting timber for the Virginia City mines. In the 1880s, when the Comstock Lode was played out, 70 to 80 cords of firewood were left piled in nearby Jones Canyon, and saws were left to rust, still imbedded in logs.

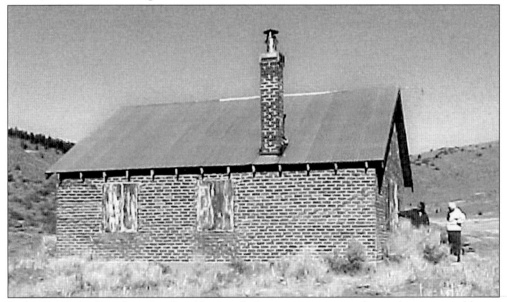

In the 1940s, the Dangberg Land and Livestock Company constructed a combination cookhouse and bunkhouse, storage cabins near the original main house, corrals, and well, so that two men could tend cattle there through the summers. One man was an irrigator, sending water over the meadows, the other was a vaquero, moving the bulls and hundreds of cows, building drift fences, and keeping the animals away from the death camas plants that gave nearby Poison Flat its name.

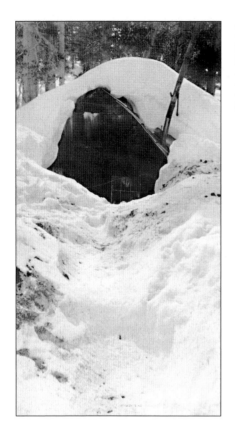

Pictured here is one of two hidden mountain cabins, five miles from Hermit Valley, used by the eccentric hermit and trapper Monte Wolf. Wolf relied on fish, venison, and bear meat to see him through winters. He told a hunter who ventured near, "Don't ever shoot a porcupine; that's my fresh meat for winter."

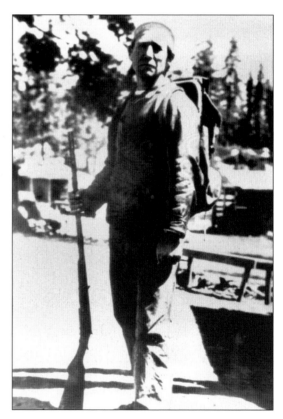

In the spring of 1940, the aging hermit left his cabin with his fishing gear and was never heard from again. (Courtesy of the Calaveras Historical Society.)

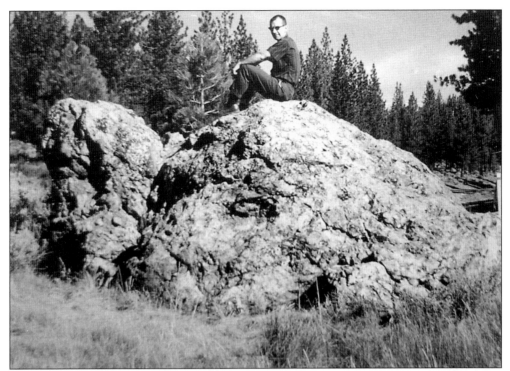

This reptilian rock was the inspiration for naming "Turtle Rock Park," near Markleeville. Although the landmark, which blocked a road-straightening project, was subsequently blown up by "unknown persons," the name remains.

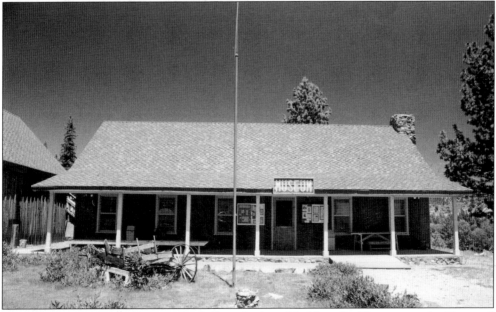

The Alpine County Museum sits on a hill overlooking Markleeville. The museum building and the old Alpine County Jail join the Old Webster Schoolhouse as the most visible landmarks in the community.

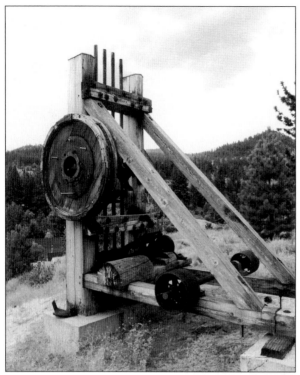

The stamp mill, originally located on Burnside Lake Road, was moved to the Alpine County Museum site in Markleeville. Although there were more than 200 mining claims in the county in 1864, most of the gold and silver ore was low grade and apt to be base. Most of the stamp mills were failures. By 1874, the *Alpine Chronicle* commented that, with the exception of the Northwestern and the Monitor, "the mines in our county are mostly idle."

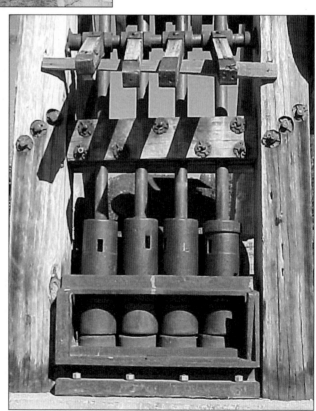

Heavy Iron "Batteries," shown here, crushed the ore prior to the smelting process.

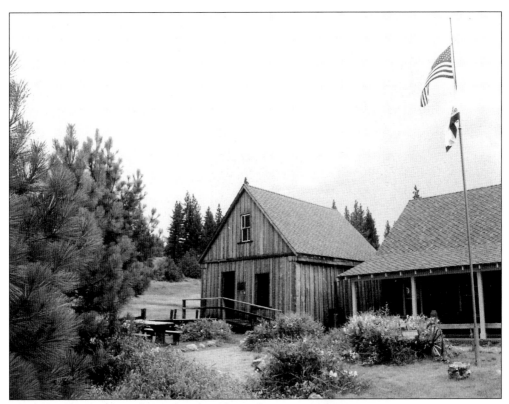

The old county jail, now located at the Alpine County Museum complex, was a controversial project from its inception. In the fall of 1866 and spring of 1867, meetings were held and "a good deal of feeling against its erection" was expressed because citizens did not wish to contract the debt. By May 18, 1867, another county newspaper, the *Weekly Bulletin,* announced that enough work had been performed for two payments to be issued.

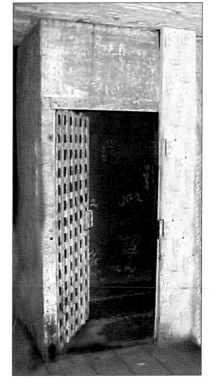

For financial reasons the original jail project was scaled back, and the quantity of iron to be used was reduced. This jail cell may reflect the fact that one of the jail's first inmates attempted to burn the building down.

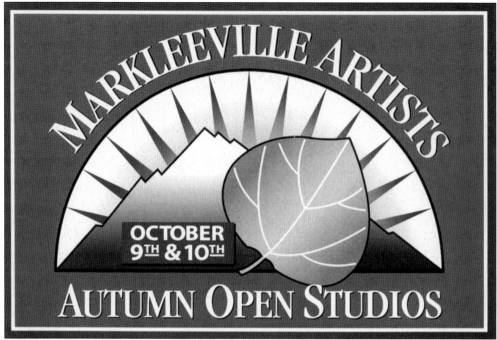

The beauty of the Alpine mountains, with their abundance of natural resources, provides ample inspiration to individuals with talent to put brush to canvas, clay to wheel, pencil to paper, chisel to stone, needle to cloth, torch to iron rod, and gems to bands of silver. The annual Markleeville Artists Autumn Open Studios event celebrates both the glorious colors of the season and the creative spirit of Alpine artists.

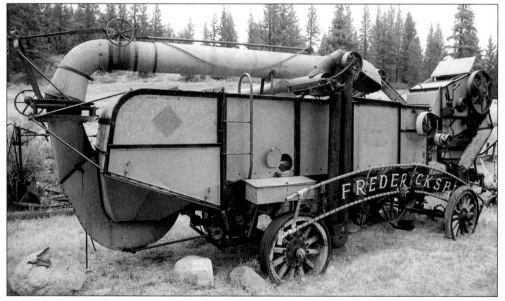

This McCormick thrashing machine, housed at the Alpine County Museum, was patented in 1907. It has solid wheels and is run by a steam donkey engine. It was used in Alpine County to harvest grain that it fed into gunny sacks. The chaff was separated and blown through the flue on top.

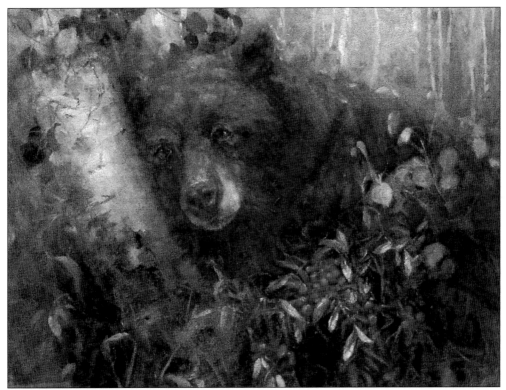

The Bear Valley Music Festival began in the summer of 1969 as a small community celebration of our classical musical heritage. It has grown over the years to feature the incredibly beautiful high Sierra setting along with the music. Festivities include a diverse offering, including folk, popular, jazz, country, full symphony orchestra, piano, and violin virtuoso performances, opera, a dance party, and a children's concert. The festival moved from the beach at Lake Alpine to the Lodge at Bear Valley and now to a tent that seats up to 1200 people. Bear Valley is probably the smallest community in the country to support a full symphony orchestra.

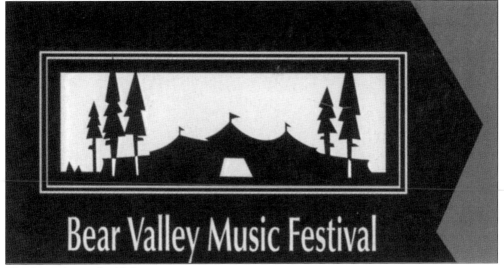

The festival runs for 16 days every summer.

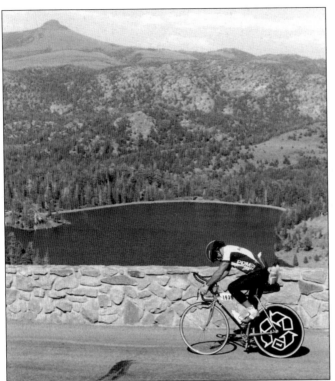

The Alpine County Death Ride, held every July and sponsored by the Alpine County Chamber of Commerce, is a testimony to the stamina and endurance of the riders, as they cycle up and over the high Sierra passes of Alpine County.

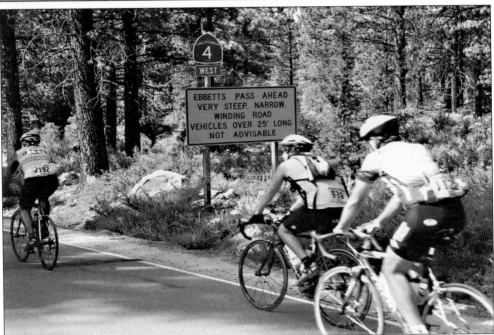

Beginning at Turtle Rock Park at an elevation of 5,500 feet, they climb to over 8,700 feet, as they ride over Monitor Pass, Ebbetts Pass, and Carson Pass. The 3,000 participants cover a total of 129 miles, climbing a total of 16,000 feet, in one day. Revenues from the event go to help support the county's nonprofit organization.